VISIONS to the TOP

— A —
Millionaire's Secret Formula
To Productivity, Visualization, And Meditation.

The **How-To Guide** For Entrepreneurs, Salespeople, and High Achievers For Wealth Creation & Dream Fulfillment

JUSTIN LEDFORD

Copyright © 2016 Justin Ledford International. All Rights Reserved. No part of this publication may be reproduced, distributed or transmitted in any form or by any means - electronic, mechanical, photocopying, recording or otherwise – without prior written permission from the publisher, except for the inclusion of brief quotations embodied in reviews and certain other non-commercial uses permitted by copyright law.

ISBN-13: 978-1533434357
ISBN-10: 1533434352

Disclaimer

This publication is designed to provide competent and reliable information regarding the subject matters covered. However, it is sold with the understanding that the author and publisher are not engaged in rendering legal, financial, or professional advice.

If legal of other expert assistance is required, the services of the professional should be sought. The author and publisher specifically disclaim any liability that is incurred from the use or application of the contents of this book.

The fact that an organization or website is referred to in this publication does not mean that the author or publisher endorses the information of that organization or website. Readers should be aware that the internet websites listed in this work may have changed or disappeared between when this work was written and when it is read.

♡ Giving Is Our Duty: 10% of author royalties are donated between three non-profit charities: The *FrontRowFoundation.org* who provide positive experiences to those braving critical health challenges, *Charitywater.org* where 100% percent of the donations go to providing clean water to people in need & *Coral.org* a 4 Star Charity that works hard to protect our most valuable and threatened ecosystem, coral reefs.

Your VIP Invitation
Visions to the Top "Visionaries" Community

This is special invitation to all fans and readers of Visions to the Top, we created a closed online community to share our Dreams, Visions and to serve as Accountability Partners. Our Dream is to help others achieve their Dreams.

Go to *www.VTTTVisionaries.com* to join the Facebook Community of other Visionaries! We look forward to seeing you there!

You can find me on:

www.JustinLedford.net
www.VisionsToTheTop.com
twitter.com/justledford

Feel free to contact me through message or a comment! See you at The Top!

Acknowledgements

Writing a book is no small effort, so I would like to thank my amazing wife who has been a huge influence and partner to all my endeavors. She read this book and helped with the edits more than anyone, she is the best partner I could ever ask for and one of the smartest people I know.

I also want to give thanks to my team who always gives their best efforts to every project. To my friends who are also my mentors, I am always learning and striving because of your friendship. And my family who always support my ventures and have given me a place to call home. Also, huge thanks for all the mentors and leaders in the personal growth community, you may not know me but I know you. Your contributions have made this world a better place. I am most thankful to The Creator who has given me the life & inspiration to follow my dreams.

Table of Contents

Introduction 1
The Test 5
Reality Check 11
Visualization 19
Intention 39
Subconscious 55
Inspiration 73
Opportunity 83
Non-Negotiables 93
Sacrifice 99
Making V.I.S.I.O.N.S Work For You 109
Time to Thrive 115

Chapter 1

Introduction

Why this book will change your life and magnify your results.

Introduction

"Vision without action is a daydream. Action without vision is a nightmare."
- Japanese Proverb

More than anything else, modern life is characterized by the seemingly relentless workplace demands we experience in our quest for success. To make matters worse, these demands are magnified by the technology which we all take advantage of – creating the expectation that we should be doing twice as much in half the time, and that we should be available 24/7. Are you tired of logging twelve hour days, sacrificing your home life as well as any other dreams you might have, only to feel that you are no further ahead than you were a year ago?

In this book, you will learn why some people achieve greatness faster than others. You will learn what lies at the root of success, and the science behind cause and effect. You will learn how to be happier and more balanced, while building an abundant life free from constant struggle and difficulties. Your best life ever will gravitate towards you, when you learn how to apply the strategies laid out in this book. You will learn how to work smart instead of hard – no longer trading all of your precious time for average outcomes.

For most of my life, I have managed to be successful in almost everything I tried. Rising to the top in all my endeavors afforded me the opportunity to talk to countless others who have also achieved greatness. What I learned from my experience and that of others is that it is a thin line which separates those who are average, from those who end up at the top of their game. The thin line over which you can step to greatness exists in every domain – regardless of what organization, business or occupation you identify most with.

Whatever you're calling in life, you will benefit from the strategies and techniques which have allowed me and countless others to generate the kind of success most only dream of. It is possible to have everything you want, while achieving balance in life. This simple How-to-Guide will help you create a plan – which, like a map, will lead you without fail to your best life ever.

Jacob, a successful entrepreneur from Texas says, "The techniques taught in this book are exactly what helped me break records in my industry. I am even able to surpass competitors with more experience. Most of the time I can see results the same day I use these techniques."

Feedback like this doesn't surprise me. The strategies set out in this guide are the ones which helped me to create a million-dollar a year company, build a marketing organization of over 4,500 people, while maintaining my position as the top producer in my division for 11 years running – all while traveling the world three months each year!

Visions To The Top is one of the most important books you'll ever read. I promise that if you follow the steps presented in the pages which follow, you will not only realize your biggest dreams faster than you ever imagined possible, you will actually work less in the process. I promise that the results you achieve will allow you to live more intentionally, freeing up time to focus on what is truly important to you and your future.

Don't be the kind of person who has dreams which will never come true. Be that person who achieves what they think is their biggest dream, and then moves on to one which is even greater. Be that person who amazes everyone who crosses their path. Be that person who leaves others wondering about how it's possible to get so much done in so little time. Be the sort of person who is motivated to take action without hesitation.

INTRODUCTION

The visualization and subconscious programming techniques and strategies you're about to learn have been tested and are proven to create lifelong results. I've shed tears, sweat, spent many hours, thousands of dollars, and late nights reading countless books in order to arrive at the essentials for success which you are about to benefit from. The steps set out for you here are simple, and the results are available to anyone who is prepared to put in the work. Follow them and commit to a journey towards the best life you can imagine.

Chapter 2
The Test

From a Disaster to a Master

The Test

> *"The journey of a thousand miles begins with one step"*
> — Lao Tzu

On November 1st 2009, life was great. No, it was amazing! At 22 years old I was a single man living the dream in a luxury apartment complex near the water. I had spent the last 4 years as the #1 distributer in my division for a $200 million marketing company, making more money than I knew how to spend. I had traveled to more places than most people travel in their lifetime. I had an awesome social life, a loving and supportive family, and the best buddies a guy could ask for. I was truly blessed.

You might say I had all a young man could want. There was no way I could have known the test that awaited me that day.

At 2:02 p.m. I was sitting on my living room floor with a 15-pound pumpkin in front of me. I had picked it up, along with some food after I left the gym. On my way home I was excited to think about how I would carve it. With endorphins flowing through my blood from my workout, sweat drying on my skin, and a smile on my face while enjoying some local music

The night before my buddies and I had been to an epic party with live music, happy people, and great dancing partners. I wanted to call my friends over to help me carve the pumpkin, but for some reason I didn't. I should have called; I had no idea how much I would be in need of their help later that day.

Physically and Mentally Tested

> *"The ultimate measure of a man is not where he stands in moments of comfort and convenience, but where he stands at times of challenge and controversy"*
> — Martin Luther King

I recall unwrapping the brand new knife from its package, taking the plastic wrapper off, slowly pulling the protective cardboard sheath off the blade, and sitting down on the floor next to the pumpkin. I remember the fan overhead circling quickly. What happened next seems surreal, like something you would see in horror movie.

I looked at the pumpkin, trying to decide where to make the first cut. I knelt on one knee for better leverage. With the knife in my right hand I inserted the blade two inches from the pumpkin's stem. My left hand was holding the pumpkin steady. The following seconds played out in slow motion.

The sharp knife which awaited my command appeared stuck, so I gave it a pull, and all of a sudden I felt heat rushing through my left hand. I stood up, wondering why it felt so hot. When I held out my hand in front of me what I saw was something you might see in a movie rated R due to graphic images!

The inside of my left hand was split open down the middle - from my thumb to the other side of my palm. I had to hold half my palm so it wouldn't fall off! I could see my pearly white bones covered in a dark red stain, and blood sprayed onto the walls, and splattered the ceiling and fan. Blood drenching my body, spraying my face to my feet. I remember saying to myself, "OK, don't freak out or you could die." With all my strength and the flowing adrenaline rush of the "fight or flight" response, I reached down to my hip area and ripped the elastic off my boxers with my right hand, tightly wrapping my wrist to slow the flow of blood.

The next moments seemed to pass quickly, but I can't recall exactly how long all this took. I ran to the bathroom, grabbed a blue towel and headed to my porch which faced the parking lot. I remember opening the door and screaming, "HELP". Two passersby laughed and pointed at me. My guess was that they thought I was pranking them because it was the day after Halloween. I was covered in blood, and my drenched towel was now the color purple as I looked up too see my friend Farrukh who had just randomly showed up.

He rushed me into his car and we flew down the road to the hospital. I stumbled out of the car only to discover that the Emergency Room door was over 200 yards away. I ran through the building and across the parking lot. A song of life and death played – there was a rhythm to my bleeding: my heart was the drum, my beating feet the sticks, and with each note that played, I bled more and more.

When I finally arrived at the reception window covered in blood and gasping for breath, a woman told me to, "go sit down, the doctors will be with you in a moment". I remember saying something along the lines of, "F*** You, I'm dying", and then rushing myself over to a set of big blue doors.

With my remaining might, I kicked the blue doors open to see doctors and nurses caring for other patients. I roared as loud as I could, "HELP ME" and everyone looked towards me. I fell to one knee, and the doctors rushed towards me.

I looked up to see a doctor starting to remove my blood soaked towel, and his facial expression spoke volumes. He then said, "What did you cut yourself with – I've never seen a cut this clean?" Remarkably my response was, "Cutco, have you heard of it?" I was still trying to sell while bleeding out!

Never Say Never

In the Emergency Room I remember lying on a bed and feeling an excruciating throbbing pain in my left hand. I recall my dad and mom being there with me. My vision was blurred and fuzzy. I caused a scene because of the pain. I was told that a cut this deep required a very specialized hand surgeon, and none were on call. An hour turned to two, three and then four hours. The pain was intense, and then nurses repeatedly injected me with morphine. My mind grew loopy as I waited for the surgeon to arrive. Doped up on opiates that were flowing through my bloodstream from an IV, I remember being silly and unusually cheerful with the nurses and doctors who laughed at my comments.

After hours of waiting the hand surgeon finally arrived. He was very rude and abrupt with me; I remember the last words that came out of my mouth while being rushed into surgery. He said to me, "You'll never use this hand again", and my response was "I do not accept your diagnosis".

I woke up what seemed like days later with those last words on my mind. Little did I know, that this incident would shape my future beliefs and habits.

Sometimes a bad situation can actually turn into the best thing that ever happens to you. Looking back on this moment in my life, I realize it created a ripple in my universe and allowed me to change for the better in so many ways. This experience changed my life forever, and is the reason that I am able to bring to you "Visions to The Top". Be prepared to soak up the rays of knowledge which follow. Consider using a highlighter and pen to capture the nuggets of wisdom which resonate most with you.

Chapter 3
Reality Check

Reality Check

"If you fail to plan you plan to fail"
— Benjamin Franklin

Rise above the Majority

Shocking evidence from the U.S. Census Bureau found out that if you take ANY 100 people and follow them through their entire working career over a 40-year period until they retire, 1 one of them will be wealthy enough to not have to worry about money in their retirement. While 4 of them will be financially in a good place, feeling secure and safe. Three will have to continue working well into the later years of their life - not for pleasure but out of necessity and 29 will be dead. A shocking 63 will have no money and will be mooching off loved ones, friends, or government hand-outs.

The reality is that only 5% of us who will be financially secure, with the ability to live life on our own terms – eating what we want, travelling as we like, and spending time with loved ones. The other 95% will have monetary hardships, struggles, and difficulties throughout their entire lives.

So, the most important question you must ask yourself, the one you must face head on is: What actions must I take today to guarantee that I don't end up like the vast majority of people; the 95% who are resigned to a life of hardship and struggle.

The truth is, the other 5% were successful because they had a roadmap. They had a vision of what they were working towards. They didn't arrive there by accident. You have to have a plan or an intention if you want to retire in the top 5%. My goal is to put a mirror in front of you so you know where you are at today and build a roadmap to where you want to be.

Breaking Free – No More Mediocrity – Joining the Top 5%

By showing up to read this book, I can immediately identify you as someone who is serious about taking life to the next level. You march to a different beat than others. The vast majority of people roll over and accept less than they could have had, been, or done. You're not OK with settling. You're done with that.

What is a level 10 life?

One of the best ways to build a sustainable roadmap to where you want to be is to know what makes you whole and complete. Are you living your level 10 life? By this I mean, are you giving time to all the things that make you a happy and fulfilled person? If you were lying on your death bed would you be at peace? Or would you have a few regrets? Don't get me wrong – it's not my intention to make anyone feel guilty. My intention is to remind you of the dreams you still have deep within your heart. Dreams that maybe you haven't shared with others. Dreams that have been forgotten.

The best thing about a level 10 life is you get to decide and rate what is most important to you. One of the best techniques I use is create a wheel of life. It reminds me of where I am at in all areas of my life and where I want to be. Below you will see an example of how this is done. You can also print a blank copy with instructions by going to www.VisionsToTheTop.com and click the resources tab. Take your time filling it out, and revisit it every so often. If you have a printer readily available print it out and fill it out, but don't wait any clean sheet of paper will do. I promise you it will be a great reminder of the importance of spending time on the things that are deeply important to you.

This was hard for me to understand when I first started out as an entrepreneur, because I didn't understand the importance of a work-life balance. I wouldn't get to spend time with family and friends. I wouldn't schedule time to take care of my health. My spiritual needs weren't being fulfilled. My wife and I wondered why we didn't have any friends.

I was so focused on business that I shut my family out, seeing them only on holidays. I was kind of a jerk. I avoided some of my best friends when they invited me to travel with them. I was losing my self and didn't even realize it.

Yes, I had money, freedom, recognition, and success - but no one to really share it with besides my wife, because she was in the same boat. The day we took the time to do this wheel was the day we looked within ourselves and discovered the things that really mattered to us. We still continue to go back to this wheel in order to re-assess and re-align what's truly important to us.

I truly believe that this wheel can help you achieve a more fulfilling life, as we did. I promise that if you fill this wheel out sincerely, and take small actions, your life will be more abundant in every aspect.

TOP TIP: When you do this wheel do it with your significant other or partner. Make a separate wheel for each of you, it will surprise you how much more you learn about each other.

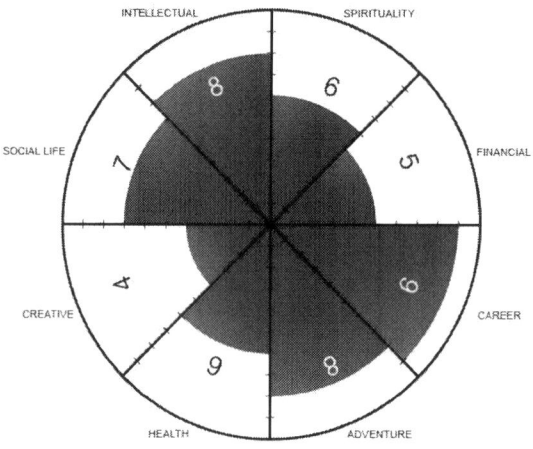

Instructions: On clean sheet of paper draw a large circle. Draw four straight lines across the circle like the photo below. Title each section with a different category. Category examples are as follows: Health, Intellectual, Social, Spirituality, Financial, Career, Adventure, and Creative. Rate your life now from 1-10 in each area, 1 being the lowest, 10 being the highest. From there you will fill/highlight each area based on the grade level you feel you are at. Finally, make a list of what you need to do to see improvement in each area, and allot time in your calendar to increase the score in each are of your life.

Remember, you can go to our website VisionsToTheTop.com and click on the resources tab to print your wheel of life out.

For Example:

Health: What is your ideal amount of exercise? What is your ideal diet? Maybe just more quiet alone time to breathe and relax?

Spirituality: Do you need to attend a ceremony more often, read scripture or be more mindful?

Social Life: What is the ideal amount of time you would like to spend with family and friends? Do you need to make new friends?

Adventure: Maybe you want to explore a new city, camping or rock climbing?

Intellectual/Personal Growth: How much time would you like to spend on your personal growth? Would you like to learn a language or skill?

Creative: Is there an instrument you have always wanted to learn? Maybe you just want to paint, write, garden, build, or sing?

Financials: How much would you like to save for retirement? Do you want to get out of debt? Would you like to give to a charity?

Career: Is there a promotion you would like to attain? A profit goal for your business?

Imagine the wheel you created as the actual wheels of a car. The air represents the score you gave that portion of your life. The only way the wheel will take you to your destination is if all of the wheel is in balance. You can't go very far with some areas being fuller than others. This wheel is a metaphor of life - when there is no balance, there is no sustainability. Use this tool to help you re-align to what's important in your life.

Creating your wheel is your first action step towards your dreams. I know it may seem like a small thing, but I promise with the techniques I am going to teach this wheel will make the next steps much easier. This wheel is one of the initial forms our coaching clients at Top Success Coaching must fill out before we can begin a session.

Your DAILY V.I.S.I.O.N.S.™

Once you know what areas need focusing on, it's easier to map out your best life ever. Now let's get to the meat and potatoes (or tofu and vegetables, for my veggie lovers) of the book.

Daily Visions is an acronym. Each letter from the acronym will be explained in its own chapter. We are going to define, show evidence, and then teach techniques that you can start to use immediately to start creating massive results.

V for **Visualizations**
I for **Intention**
S for **Subconscious**
I for **Inspiration**
O for **Opportunity**
N for **Non-Negotiables**
S for **Sacrifices**

When you have absolute clarity, precise focus, and belief that it can be done, you will achieve your dreams. Once you have these, nothing can stop you, unless you take your eyes off the prize. We all know where attention goes is where energy flows. It is rare to hit a target you can't see. If you tap into your DAILY V.I.S.I.O.N.S and are willing to put in the work, you will see massive results in all areas of your life.

Chapter 4
Visualization

Visualization

"Create a vision of who you want to be, and then live into that picture as if it were already true."
- Arnold Schwarzenegger

Visualization, also known as mental rehearsal or imagery, involves using all of the senses to create or recreate an event or image in the mind. This is a multisensory endeavor which allows you to tap into your inner world in order to create positive results in your outer world. As T Harv Eker said, "If you want to change the fruits, you will first have to change the roots. If you want to change the visible, you must first change the invisible".

The Case for Visualization

Russian scientists Ellen Rogin and Lisa Kueng published a study on the effects of visualization. They studied four groups of Olympic athletes, having each group do a different combination of mental and physical training. The results were mind blowing!

Group1: 100% physical training only
Group 2: 75% physical training, 25% mental training
Group 3: 50% physical training, 50% mental training
Group 4: 25% physical training, 75% mental training

Which group do you think performed the best during the Olympics? Well, if you picked Group 4 you're correct! The USA Olympic committee was so impressed by these results that they decided to increase their full time staff of psychologists from one to over a dozen. Other nations understand the power of visualization and mental imagery as well, and many now also bring a team of psychologists to the Olympics to help athletes practice visualization.

Success Leaves Clues

Kerri Walsh and Misty May-Treanor are dominating the volleyball world. These ladies are one of the most successful duos to ever play the sport. In fact, they have won Olympic Gold Medals three times. Walsh told USA Today in an interview: "We often rely on meditation, yoga, and visualization. A lot of what we do is visualization, to be able to … take in the sights, the sounds, the stress, the excitement — that's going to serve us really well moving forward."

Throughout his life, Arnold Schwarzenegger has practiced visualization. He said that early in his bodybuilding: "I had this fixed idea of growing a body like Reg Park's. The model was there in my mind; I only had to grow enough to fill it." He explained, "The more I focused in on this image and worked and grew, the more I saw it was real and possible for me to be like him." After finding rapid success in his practice, Arnold realized he could use this power of belief through visualizing his reality for whatever goals he wanted. Later in his life he employed mental rehearsal to achieve success in acting and politics. Schwarzenegger said he utilized these same mental tricks: "It's the same process I used in bodybuilding: What you do is create a vision of who you want to be — and then live that picture as if it were already true."

Like so many successful people, Oprah Winfrey started from humble beginnings - living with her grandma who struggled to make ends meet. She would tell herself "My life won't be like this. My life won't be like this; it will be better." Little did she know, she was creating magnetic forces for her future. On "The Oprah Winfrey Show" she discussed the importance of creating a vision board to the realization of dreams. One of my favorite pieces of wisdom from Oprah is "Create the highest, grandest vision possible for your life, because you become what you believe."

Visualization is a practice well known to most elite athletes, entrepreneurs, writers, celebrities, and some of the most successful people to ever live.

You've probably heard the sayings "Seeing is believing" or "What you focus on expands." The practice of closing your eyes and seeing your dreams as you intend them in your mind is very powerful and should be practiced every day. Visualization or Mental Rehearsal is an elite tool for personal development.

A quick poem from me to you

Imagine for a second these quotes have found you exactly at this perfect moment in time,
some from decades ago and some closer in time,
here to remind you as a guide.
We sometimes forget to post personal growth quotes up on the wall,
so here are a few of my favorites to inspire all.
Below is your sign, wealth and wisdom in a handful of influential words, with the hopes that you will begin your practice and align.
Slow your breath or your mind will be tangled like a vine.
Clarity and focus allows you to feel connected to the divine.
If practiced regularly you can achieve bliss and feel high as cloud nine.

Powerful Visualization Quotes to Reflect On

1 – "If you want to reach a goal, you must see the reaching in your own mind before you actually arrive at your goal."

– Zig Ziglar

Interesting brain studies have found that practicing visualization produces the same mental instruction as actually doing the actions. During your mental rehearsal you are actually re-wiring your nervous system - empowering yourself and making the daily task which move you towards your goal easier. Studies have shown that visualization exercises can magnify your motor performance, elevate your internal motivation, boost your confidence, and increase your energy. Simply put – they help align you with your dreams and goals. Staying on course on the journey towards becoming your best version of yourself can be challenging. However, applying visualization techniques and seeing yourself achieving each goal or dream certainly will make life more fun and fulfilling, as well as giving you the sustained energy needed to stay on course. Later in the chapter I will show you the simplest way to activate your visions.

>   *2 – "To bring anything into your life imagine that it's already there"*
>   **-Richard Bach**

Every morning after my prayer I visualize myself at that moment of victory, the moment I intend to achieve. For example, in my sales business my goal is to continue to be the top performer in my division. So here is what I'll visualize as if it's already there. I see and feel my footsteps while walking onto the stage, standing there with my gorgeous wife, accepting the recognition from the region president. I tap into what's around me. In front of me, I see bright lights and the audience smiling at me and hear cheering and clapping. To the right there is a big screen with my sales number, indicating what I sold for the year in big bold letters! I'm holding onto my wife's hand. I feel her touch, and we're both smiling. I feel the emotions of happiness, gratitude, and excitement. Before I end my visualization I intensify these emotions and turn them up. I open my eyes and start my day moving towards the direction of this dream. Later in this book I'll explain a technique for turn up your "dial", to increase your emotions.

> *3 – "When one starts to visualize the impossible one begins to see it as possible"*
> **– Cherie Carter Scott**

Your inner mental pictures will create your outer world's reality. Visualization will help increase your belief in yourself, as well as your confidence in achieving a particular goal. How abundant do you want your life to be? The goals you set for yourself and visualize daily will be realized as long as you're willing to get up and work.

> *4- "I would visualize things coming to me. It would just make me feel better. Visualization works if you work hard. That's the thing. You can't just visualize and go eat a sandwich."*
> **– Jim Carrey**

Although visualization is one of the most elite techniques I have ever been introduced to, if a person doesn't combine it with massive action daily, then nothing will happen. When you mix intensified emotions into your visualization practice, then take action and believe that you will achieve your goal, you will begin to see miracles unfold in your life. My friends across the country who practice visualization BLOW the sales numbers of others. Every year for the last 11 years, I have been the #1 rep in my division. I attribute this blessing to the focused visualization which I practice every morning.

> *5 - "I came to realize that visualizing, projecting yourself into a successful situation, is the most powerful means there is of achieving personal goals"*
> **- Leonard Lauder**

Along with his wife, Leonard Lauder, the American businessman who founded The Estée Lauder Companies has impacted and enriched the lives of millions of people around the globe. His net worth is over $9.6 Billion! His amazing words of wisdom should remind you of the personal power that lies within yourself. Visualization is the most powerful tool that those at the top use to achieve their goals.

Your Visions Are Your Dreams

> *"The future belongs to those who believe in the beauty of their dreams"*
> – **Eleanor Roosevelt**

People sometimes get so caught up with work, TV shows, and daily habits that they forget to dream. When is the last time you wrote down five dreams in one sitting? Good for you if you've done so recently, but most people haven't done this in a while, if ever. Whatever the case, it's important to understand your dreams equal your vision and that your DAILY V.I.S.I.O.N.S.™ equal your dreams.

Your vision is what gives you power. It is the gift of seeing into your future before it happens. It is what helps you to know with certainty that you will achieve the dreams inside of your heart. Consider Oprah's words when she said, "Create the highest, grandest vision possible for your life, because you become what you believe." Look at her now she just surpassed a net worth of 3 billion dollars.

Building Dreams

Every day you take actions that will either bring you closer to or further from your dreams. Always question whether you are building a pathway to your dreams. Imagine your dreams as bricks which are building a pathway. At the beginning of each day, you should mentally map out the completion of the

VISUALIZATION

pathway to your dreams. Taking action is like laying a brick on your pathway, but when you combine action with visualization you are laying multiple bricks. Before you know it you will have a complete pathway. Later in the book I will go over the importance of tapping into your senses during your visualization practice.

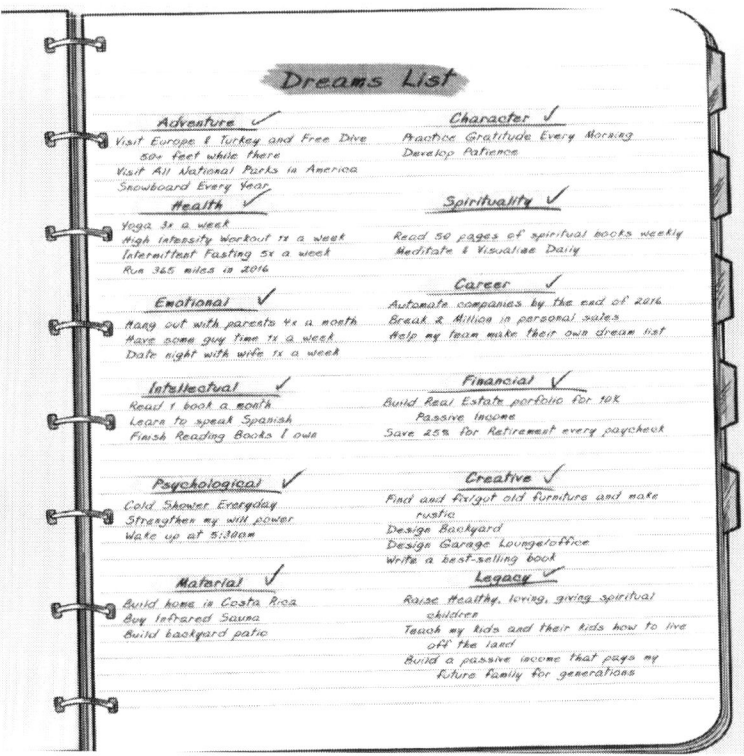

Why People Forget Their Dreams

What sounds like more fun to you? Living a life of mediocrity, uncertainty, being stressed out or worried, thinking thoughts of I'm not sure I can, I don't know if... I can't do... I wish I could... OR living a life of abundance and gratitude, being happy, being content, being focused on an objective, thinking thoughts of I believe I can achieve this. I know this is possible, I will... I am ready... I can... I look forward to... Obviously the latter sounds more fun, fulfilling, and inspiring. The type of life you live is determined by the thoughts you think. I will show you how to replace bad thoughts with good ones.

If I could I define the word faith in one single word it would be "Belief". Belief is beyond powerful! I was told once that F.E.A.R stands for False Evidence Appearing Real and F.A.I.T.H stands for Fully Anticipating It to Happen! One of personal favorite motivational speakers and author Tony Robbins said: "What's the difference between fear & faith? Both are made up. Fear is imagination undirected & faith is your power to direct imagination."

Visualization Is Nothing New

This science of visualization is as old as man himself. Ancient men of wisdom knew about it and used it. Today writers translated the subject of energy into a language which we can all understand. T Harv Eker said, "Our inner world creates our outer world". I am living proof that our inner thoughts and beliefs about something are directly correlated to our reality. My recognition as the #1 rep in my division for 11 years straight, building a over million dollar a year company, or developing an organization of over 4,500 individuals is not the result of luck, or the waving of a magic wand.

It is the result of the rituals which I practice every morning in order to rewire my subconscious every day. I visualize and see myself in front of happy customers, I imagine and see positive sharp individuals entering my office for a position, I see myself on stage winning the trophy, I hear applause, and I intensify the emotions of happiness, gratitude, and joy in my practice at each moment of future success I seek.

TOP TIP: Here is a secret tip during visualization. Try feeling what you would feel in that moment of victory, that moment of success you are seeking. Feel that feeling and amplify it

Once while working at a trade show I befriended a booth neighbor named Mike, who was selling a unique portable fan created for golf carts and boats which had been invented by his wife. Mike was in his 60's, and wealthy enough to own custom built homes in places like Aspen, Colorado and Woodlands, Texas. During our conversations he told me about his career in the industrial power plant business and how he has created over 21 patents in this industry. His personal business generates over $60 million a year in sales. I asked him about what he considered to be the most important factors which contributed to his success. His answer? Visualization, Mental Rehearsal and hard work!

From an outsider's perspective you might wonder "why not retire and just chill?" So I asked him just that. His response was priceless. "That would be so boring", he said, "I love to create, design and build the life of my dreams. If we stop growing, we begin dying. Energy is always moving, never staying still. Why would I want to stay still"? This statement really struck a chord with me. By tapping into our inner world through meditation and visualization, we tap into the realm of infinite possibilities. We all have the potential to create our dream life. Later in this book I will explain how intention plays a crucial role in your visualization process.

Your Mind Is Made for This

Srinivasan Pillay, scientist, Harvard M.D and the author of "Your Brain and Business: The Neuroscience of Great Leaders," says, "We stimulate the same brain regions when we visualize an action as we do when we actually perform that same action," basically you reprogram your brain to achieve whatever it wants. For this practice to work you must first determine your goal, visualize achieving this goal in vivid detail daily, and take action towards these goals every day.

These are just a few examples of top performers using positive visualization techniques. There are so many others that openly credit it as a success strategy. Your best life ever is hidden inside of you, waiting to be released. The answers to your most cherished hopes, and deepest questions are waiting to be found. All you have to do is look inward. A seed planted, watered, and given enough sun-shine grows into a beautiful fruit tree. Your amplified visual thoughts are those seeds, your daily practice of visualization is the water, and the action you take daily is the sun shine giving those dreams the nutrients they need to grow to fruition.

Visions are like seeds for your life. What seed dreams are you ready to manifest?

When you think of BIG, hairy, audacious goals that you want to accomplish, it is possible to have self-doubt or get concerned about all the obstacles that will come your way. One piece of advice is never let that obstacle fool you into settling for mediocrity. We've all heard the saying: how do you eat a whole elephant? Just take one bite at a time. Keep moving forward, obstacles will come - just make adjustments and get back on the path straight towards your dreams or goals.

How-To: Use Mental Imagery

Everybody is at different stages and/or is wired different when it comes to visualization. There are different techniques for using mental imagery. You can use single or multiple images.

Single Image: Focusing on a single image related to your future goal, you hold that image in your mind and tap into the different feelings and senses while there.

Multiple Images: Focusing on multiple images related to your future goal, you hold these multiple images in your mind and tap into the different feelings and senses while there. This is my preferred method.

If you are new at the practice of visualization, start off with using a single image technique for your goal, focusing on something which illustrates you achieving this goal.

If you are more experienced in the practice of visualization, I suggest you use the multiple images practice and increase your feelings while you are doing so.

Whichever method you use; the next time you practice visualization imagine yourself exactly one year from now as if you are looking back in time. Think about the feeling of accomplishment which goes hand in hand with achieving your goal. Ask yourself "Where will I be a year from now?" "How will I feel when I achieve my goal?" "What emotions come up at that moment of success one year from now?" Tap into in those emotions and that one image.

By getting in the habit of tapping into where you will be one year from now and going to that spot you will be rewiring your subconscious – increasing your belief in yourself and seeing your success as possible. Some people think this is some kind of magic trick. I disagree - this is not magic; it is the power of belief. When a person starts to believe that they can achieve their goal, and then takes the necessary actions towards doing so, "miracles" begin to show up in various forms. You begin to meet the right people, find yourself in the right situations, and experience the right coincidences.

Don't get tricked into the new age philosophy which encourages visualize the goal and expect it to come to you without work. Your dreams and goals come to you when your inner world is in alignment with what you seek. You have to become the person that is ready for that goal. It takes daily action and daily repetitive visualization. That daily visualization is what waters the seeds and allows them to take strong roots in your life. Your action is what will turn your dreams into goal attainment.

How-To: Amplify & Intensify Visualization

Imagine for a moment that you have a dial located on your chest – one which can be turned up and down from 1 to 10. When working your way through the 5 phases of visualization, imagine turning up this dial to increase the frequency of emotion associated with your images. This will allow you to experience your emotions more intensely. Have you ever been so happy you've cried? How you ever felt so in love that you were filled with joy? The emotions you want to choose are those of happiness, joy, certainty, confidence, gratitude or any other positive emotions which make you feel good.

Turn up your emotional dial during your visualization practice, and you will be able to create a frequency or energy that matches the moment of victory you envision. You will be tapping into the reality of that dream you wish to come true. By doing this every day, and putting forth the required effort - guess what happens? Your dream will come true EVERYTIME, as long as you're willing to take daily action.

How-To: Use the 5 Phase Visualization Exercise

1. Inward Breath - Go into a quiet place away from distractions, sit down and begin to relax. Take a deep breath, calm your mind, calm you heart, just relax. Close your eyes. Inhale deeply through your nose with the intention that you are filling up your Vagus nerve - a nerve that runs through heart to your lungs. Each exhale should come from the back of your throat, as if you're trying to fog up a mirror. You will feel a tingly feeling in your head from being filled with oxygen. Continue this type of breathing throughout the phases 1-5. (Take as long as you like - I like to do this breathing for a minute or so.)

2. Past visions - With your eyes still closed, start to visualize and feel moments from your past accomplishments. Run through several happy, positive moments from your past, while you continue the phase 1 breathing. These moments can be any moment that brought you joy - time with your kids, a past achievement, a fun adventure, a passionate moment with your spouse. You are priming your mind to believe it can see future visions.

(Take as long as you like - I like to focus on past visions for at least 2 minutes or longer.)

3. Future Visions - With your eyes still closed, begin to transition your mental imagery from past to future dreams. Visually see and feel those future moments in time as if you are accomplishing them. These future moments can be anything that you are excited to achieve or any moment you look forward to. Tap into multiple
senses. What do you hear? What do you see around you? What positive emotions do you feel internally at that moment? Is there something you can touch? Is there something you can smell at that moment of victory? (Take as long as you like while in future visions. This is normally the longest section for me, lasting 2-10 minutes - sometimes more.)

4. Turn Up the Frequency - With your eyes still closed and your phase 1 breathing, continue to focus on future visions, while turning up your emotional dial. If you're feeling grateful turn it to a level 10 gratitude. If you're feeling excited turn it up to a level 10 excitement. If you feel blessed intensify this emotion to a level 10. Increase the frequency of the energy associated with the reality you want and you cannot help but succeed. Although your eyes are closed, your physiology will change when you begin turning up the frequency. Put a huge smile on your face, put your hands on your heart, rock back and forth. Really turn up the dial. (Turn up your dial while focused on future visions. See this phase like a sprint at the end of the race. Remaining focused on your image of the future, turn it up for as long as you can. This section is normally pretty quick for me - 20-30 seconds per image.)

5. Tap into The Cosmos - Once you get to this phase, you're almost done. With your eyes still closed, and continuing your phase 1 breathing – end your visions. Try to see nothing but black space. Feel only the vast infinite space inside of yourself. Set your intention to being ready to accept any blessings which may come your way. Guide your spirit to say, "I'm ready to receive these dreams". "I'm grateful for what's coming my way". Once you feel calm and collected open your eyes and start your day. (Take as long as you like tap into the Cosmic Energy, God's Infinite Power, or whatever it is that you strongly believe in. Do this for a minute or so and flood your mind with acceptance and gratitude of what will be coming your way.)

The Power of Belief

Belief that you will achieve your dream is an integral part of giving your visions power. If you don't believe you can manifest your dreams, then what makes you think you will? It's OK to have doubt, but that doubt came from somewhere deep within your subconscious mind and can be reconfigured. A child never says "I'm not the kind of person who could…" because they haven't learned to limit their full potential, have not yet been filled with the pessimistic musings of others. That little voice that doesn't think you can do x, y, or z is not from you. It is from some person, a TV show, a song, a bully at school. It is a voice from the past.

TOP TIP: If you have a task that will help you towards your goal but you don't feel like doing it, take this as a sign that it is the action you need to do most right now. By attacking those weak thoughts with action you will drown out weakness with your warrior mentality. Nothing beats weak thoughts like taking action. Taking these simple actions helps to reprogram your mind and makes you more decisive, bold, and strong mentally.

Vision Casting

Your emotions and how you feel about your goal are the magnetic forces that exist in the space between your dreams and where you are now. One of the best ways to stay connected with your dreams is through a vision board. A vision board is a place where you cut out or copy and paste images related to your dreams. By placing this board somewhere you'll see it regularly, you will be able to maintain your focus on specific goals. It's a simple tool which can have a momentous effect on your subconscious mind. A vision board helps combat the human tendency to become easily distracted, as well as targeting forgetfulness, and addressing the reality that modern life is very busy. Making use of a vision board serves several purposes.

- ▶ Put a bullseye on your goal and gives it clarity
- ▶ Reminds you to be attentive to your intentions
- ▶ Reinforces the mental pictures and emotions your visualization practice
- ▶ Reminds you to WORK and TAKE MASSIVE ACTION towards your goals

When you see photos which represent your greatest dreams pasted on your vision board, you will signal your mind to flex the necessary muscles which will move you towards that vision. The words and images that make up your vision board should represent your top priorities in life. Having a vision board present and readily available will help combat the mental fatigue which you will inevitably experience along the way. Your vision board is a physical blueprint of your heart's desires. With it, the dreams and feelings residing in your subconscious will make themselves known to your conscious mind. Most people put their vision board in their room, office or as a wallpaper on their laptop or computer. Just make sure to place it where you can see it often.

Vision Boards Make Dreams a Reality

Sipping a cup of organic coffee made through a double wall, stainless French press set the stage for an interesting conversation I had with one of my best friends Trevor. We were discussing the chain of events that led him and his wife Lesa to acquire their beautiful new ranch style home in Arizona, and his story illustrates the power of vision casting. They created a vision board together, and placed it on the ceiling above their bed. Every morning, and every evening they would look up and see images of their dreams dancing overhead. Figuring prominently amongst the photos on their vision board, they included the words "Imagine your Home". He explained that just two months earlier they didn't think it possible to have a home such as the one they had recently acquired, but with the help of a vision board, their dream became a reality.

Another example of the power of vision boards comes from a young man named Matt. During his junior year of college, Matt worked twelve hours a semester for a company who gave Rolex watches to its' highest achievers. Matt decided to set himself the huge goal of being in the less than 1% of salespeople who received such an award. He began to manifest this dream – waking up and going to bed thinking about wearing a ROLEX™ on his wrist. He told everyone he came in contact with that he would win this prize. He had photos of a Rolex on his phone, and scattered phrases posted on his calendar! He achieved his goal and won the Rolex. The point is, the more you see your dream the easier it is to pursue it.

"To succeed in business, you need to make others see your vision."
-John Henry Patterson

A final illustration of the successful use of a vision board comes from a conversation that my wife and I had with a friend over dinner. Teddy is a very successful real estate investor, with a home in an affluent Houston neighborhood, and a driveway lined with nice cars including a Bentley. He and I laughed and talked about life, goals, dreams, and good times. We were sitting at the kitchen table as the night wound down, when he laughed as he began to tell us about his vision board experience.

When Teddy was only 20 years old he had a vision board containing images of a Mercedes, nice watches, future vacations, and various phrases. He got excited talking about the subject and mentioned that he still uses a vision board today, as it helps him to maintain a laser focus. As he achieved each and every goal he set for himself, his life became more fulfilling. It was not only about what he had managed to acquire, but about the person he had become through the process, and the lives which he had impacted along the journey.

We all know people who are just drifting through life, going through the motions, following the crowd, going to work, coming home, turning on the TV, going to bed and repeating that process over again the next day. You are not living your dreams if you are just being carried along through life.

Vision boards will help to bring your dreams and goals into focus, so begin to think of them as glasses to someone whose eyesight is blurry.

> *"Dreams can only become reality when they become your vision."*
> – Dave Ramsey

Here is an example of my vision board, placed in a location I see multiple times a day. I recommend you schedule time today or this week to make yours.

Below are some questions you can ask yourself before you begin your online image search. Your answers will dictate what images you will want to look for. Select your images, copy, paste, print, and place on your vision board. You may also send your images to an office supply store and have them print in high quality paper for you. Simple as that! Now your inner desires will be in the forefront of your mind every day.

What kind of vehicles do you want to own?
Where would you like to travel to?
How would your dream house to look like?
What kind of wardrobe would you like to have?
What hobbies do you love?
What goals do you want to achieve this year?
Who or what organizations would you be interested in helping?

Chapter 5
Intention

Intention

"Our intention creates our reality"
                                    -Wayne Dyer

A working definition of "intention" is: the end or object intended; a purpose, an aim or a plan.

Please understand that we get what we intend. Each and every human being has a magnetic force within which, if activated, can help them create the life of their dreams. The activation switch is your personal power of intention. People that achieve greatness in their life don't just get there by chance or accident. They were very intentional when they started their process, and they kept that intention alive as proceeded. Many people start on a particular path, and then fall off it because they neglected to stay in touch with their intention. There are many things you need to know about intention, and once you are done with this chapter you will begin to observe important things about yourself.

Early in my childhood I became fascinated with frequencies, energy, electricity, vibrations and magnetic forces. I would read, watch videos, and experiment with these concepts. I used to play with electrical fences and try to create sparks - something about it always drew me to learn more.

Later in life I grew to believe that everything, including our thoughts, is energy. Nikola Tesla who was largely responsible for developing the AC electrical system said, "If you want to find the secrets of the universe think in terms of energy, frequency, and vibration." Einstein also believed in the supremacy of energy saying, "Everything is energy and that is all there is to it. Match the frequency of the reality you want and you cannot help but get that reality. It can be no other way. This is not philosophy. This is Physics."

The Proof is in The Water

To understand your personal power within let's take a look at an incredible scientific study by Dr. Masaru Emoto. This study revealed that our words and thoughts can impact every cell in our body! Let me say that again. The words you say and the thoughts you think can change every cell in your body. Think about this for a second.

As over 70% of the human body consists of water, Dr. Emoto decided to study the correlation between intentions, words, and sounds to see if these had any effect on the molecular structure of water. Using cryogenic temperatures his experiments evidenced incredible results. Water molecules literally changed their shapes and structures when exposed to various words. Positive words such as: love, gratitude, and hope, consistently produced physically attractive crystals. These crystals were aesthetically pleasing to look at, with structures like beautiful, symmetric snowflakes. Negative words like hate, stupid, and fool contributed to the foundation of water crystals that were repulsive to look at - resembling poorly formed blobs.

Heavy metal music discombobulated the molecules and made them look like diseased, shapeless forms, with brown and red colors despite the clarity of water. Beethoven melodies, on the other hand, transformed water molecules into gorgeous crystals – white in color, with intricate designs.

What sounds are you exposing yourself to? Is it possible that the words we speak and hear, as well as the images we see, can impact our cells on a molecular level? If words can change the physical structure of a molecule, imagine what the power of intention can do.

Let's take a look at Dr. Emoto's next study. He gathered 2,000 participants in Tokyo and led them in a 5 minute positively intended prayer of gratitude. The prayer was directed at water bottles located 5,000 miles away in an electromagnetically shielded, double-steel-walled room at the Institute of Noetic Sciences (IONS) in Petaluma, California. Crazy as it sounds, when the samples arrived back at his lab in Tokyo the results were irrefutable. Viewed under a microscope, the water which had been reinforced with pleasant intention yielded beautiful crystal structures. Normal water with no positive intention sent its' way, experienced no molecular changes. The power of intention can overcome all barriers, and distance.

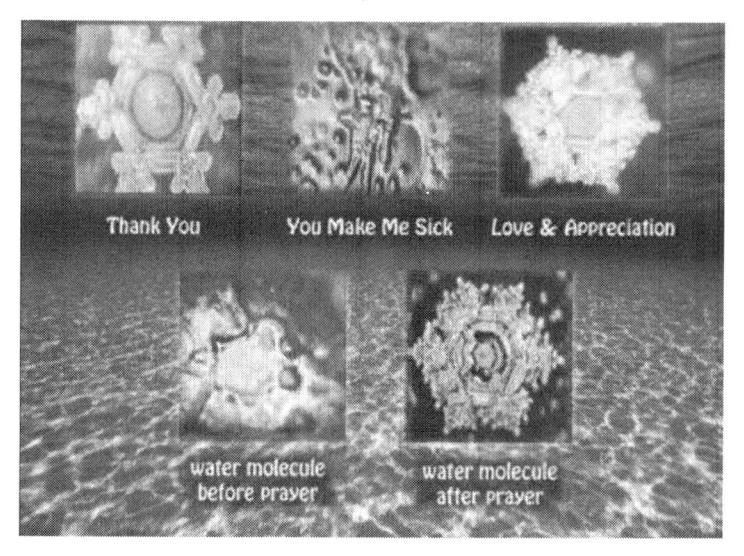

Thank You   You Make Me Sick   Love & Appreciation

water molecule before prayer   water molecule after prayer

Mind over Matter

I am a firm believer that the reason I can move my hand is because of the mental strength I gained after walking on blistering hot coals at an Anthony Robbins seminar. At that weekend seminar, I became convinced that anything is possible if you believe you can do it. I asked myself dozens a times a day: "What's the best exercise I can to do heal faster?" "How can I become even healthier and heal faster?" I told myself: "My hand is strong and works perfectly" "I am healing machine". I truly believed everything I told myself, even when the pain was great, or when the medical reports said otherwise.

I intended that I would be fine. My positive belief kept me strong and focused, and this provided me with a warrior mindset. Every day I practiced my own physical therapy, doing my best to move each finger. Slowly but surely I began to wiggle my fingers. Yes, the pain was real -but I knew I had to think positively, focusing on getting my hand back to normal, rather than on the pain. I decided to go back to work that week, and found people to drive me.

Within three months I was moving all my fingers. In six months I could close my hand. By the nine-month mark, I was lifting light weights again! Remember the hand surgeon who said I'd never use my hand again? I proved him wrong! My mind was more powerful than all the medical reports. Intention is the fuel that makes your motor run. Daily action is your motor. Believing in yourself and in the process is what keeps you going, and gets you to your destination.

Belief moves mountains!

The people in a very small Indian village had to walk 8 miles around a mountain every day to get to the nearest town. That town housed the nearest school, hospital, market and drinking water. For many years the people of the village repeatedly asked their government to cut a road through the mountain, but in such a poor rural area there was no funding to support such a massive project. There was a woman named Faguni Devi whose habit it was to walk to the larger town for water. One day on her journey she tripped, and shortly after this incident died, because she could not be delivered to the hospital in time. Understandably, her husband Dasrath Manjhi could deal with this situation no longer. His moment of despair created a spark within him, igniting a chain of events that would impact the lives of millions of people.

That very day, Dasrath set his intention to carve out a road himself, so that no one from that village would have to suffer the way his wife and he had. Dasrath sold his goats to buy a hammer, chisel, and crowbar. The townspeople ridiculed him and thought he was going crazy. He would chip away at the mountain with his hammer before he went to work on his farm. As Dasrath began to make progress, the people in his village began to believe in his efforts, and supported him by tools and food. Twenty-two years later, over 60 villages benefit from Dasrath's handmade road which cuts straight through the mountain.

My wish for you is that you be able to drown out all dream snatchers, the nay-sayers, the haters. Don't listen to the disbelief of others. Let them disbelieve - if they are around when you accomplish your goal you will notice their silence! There will always be people who tell you that you can't accomplish this or that goal. In my life, I choose to eliminate these people from my life, and if I can't, I find a way to distance myself from these folks. I recommend that you do the same!

Protect Your Castle

> *"You are the average of the people you spend the most time with"*
>
> – Jim Rohn.

Picture this: Inside of you there is a secret castle, vast in abundance, containing everything you can desire. It is beautifully decorated – built from carved stone, and containing majestic fountains, golden brick pathways, and fabulous gardens. Protecting your castle is a moat; which surrounds the perimeter, and contains deep water full of alligators and piranhas waiting to make a meal of anything that falls in. There is only one bridge over the moat, and it leads to the main entrance. You must protect your bridge and only allow in that which is helpful to your castle. Anything harmful should never be permitted to enter. If it does, things can go horribly wrong.

This castle is a metaphor for your subconscious mind. We must guard our minds and be protective of what we allow to enter. Our thoughts and the words that cross the bridge manifest as our reality. These same thoughts and words have the power to either move you towards or distance you from your goal.

When I was a child, my mom lived near the sea in a small town called Surfside. We would spend many a warm, sunny days on the beach fishing, crabbing, surfing and relaxing with the family. Our nights were spent stargazing and relaxing by a bonfire. I remember that my mother would often take us crabbing, to catch something for a wonderful dinner. In the high season, we would fill our buckets with blue crab. I noticed that our catch was not secure in the basket – crabs have the ability to climb out. Once the basket was full however, some crabs will pull the leg of the one trying to escape.

Do you have crabs in your life that might be holding you back from growing and not helping you get to your destination?

I truly believe this. I go out of my way to spend time with those who are more successful than I am. It can be uncomfortable at first, but I noticed that I grew more and was more fulfilled because doing so helped me to align with my own personal goals. I know that some people may find it hard to surround themselves with those who will lift them up. When I first started on a journey of personal growth and development, I didn't have a powerful circle of influence to connect with. As an alternative, I would listen to audiotapes, and read books about people who inspired me. Slowly, I began to attract the right people in my life. You can do the same in order to inspire yourself, and help lift yourself out of that crab bucket.

To become the best version of yourself you need to spend your time with those who elevate you, help you thrive, push you towards your dreams, and who speak words of positive encouragement. If you want to fly with the eagles, you can't flock with the seagulls.

Although awesome creatures, seagulls are just not programmed to soar as high as eagles. The human species is no different, except we have the advantage of choice. We can program ourselves to fly high in our journey of life, achieving great heights, or hang out on the coast and accept whatever comes our way. We have to be intentional with what we are allowing into our minds, how we are taking care of our bodies, and be cautious of who we are letting in our circle. Ultimately we become who we associate with, so be intentional about deciding who gets to share in your life energy.

Intentional spoken words

"Whether you think you can, or can't your right."
– Henry Ford

As a young entrepreneur I learned the power of words and how they can influence every aspect of our life. They can impact how we feel, act and even how we perform. This seems like a very basic premise, yet many people seem unaware of it. The words we speak effect every cell in our bodies, in either a positive or negative fashion. Some words empower you, while others have the ability to disempower you. In order to be in constant pursuit of our highest self we have to be intentional with the words we speak. Below are some examples of empowering, and disempowering speech.

Empowering words
- I am going to hit my goal this year
- I know the importance of personal growth
- I will have the best month of my life
- I believe in taking massive action daily

Disempowering words

I can't…	- Maybe…
I'm doing ok; I guess…	- I don't know…
I am not…	- I never…

When choosing language, there is a general rule of thumb to follow. Whatever follows the word "I" will have the power to dictate your feelings and actions. By replacing disempowering words with empowering ones, we have the ability to change the outcome of any situation.

Quantum mechanics describes the relationship between cause and effect, and its' principles demonstrate how thoughts can change outcomes. Often described as the "science of the very small", Quantum Mechanics endeavors to explain the behavior of matter as it interacts with energy on the scale of atoms and subatomic particles. All matter, including thought, are characterized by different energy vibrations. Therefore, intentionally choose powerful thoughts, as these will influence your outcomes.

Power of Gratitude

In another study on the power of intention, Dr. Emoto placed cooked rice in one of three containers. The first container was told "thank you," the second container was told "you're an idiot," and the third container was completely ignored. The results were amazing. Thirty days after the words were spoken to the rice, it was found that the rice in the first container gave off a strong pleasant odor and remained white in color. That in the second container turned black, while the neglected rice had grown moldy and was beginning to rot away.

What do the results of this rice study imply? Grateful positive intentions foster life, rude, hateful intentions destroy it, and apathy results in a slow decay. So, adopt an attitude of gratitude and watch your life change. Your life will be longer, more enjoyable, and easy on the eyes!

Gratitude Mindset

Be grateful for everything in your life. If you woke up on this side of the grave, it is a day to celebrate - there is a reason you're still here, and you have a purpose to fulfill on earth. I believe the main reason you're alive is to "become the best version" of yourself.

It has been said that gratitude is one of the most powerful emotions the heart and mind can harness. It is impossible to feel fear, and anger while feeling grateful. Can you remember a time your heart was filled with gratitude, but was angry as well? This is not possible – gratitude is the antithesis of anger.

Anytime you need a reality check or a pick me up - try gratitude! Anytime you're feeling down, be grateful and your spirits will be lifted. Here is a little tip which can launch you into a positive mindset immediately. Ponder this for a moment: if you have a roof over your head, food to eat and clothes to wear, how amazing is your life already? There are literally millions of people on this planet with none of these blessings. We should tap into gratitude every day and remember to count our blessings.

TOP TIP: The moment you wake up, immediately think about three things you're grateful for. The emotions which your gratitude generates will help you have a more positive and fulfilling day.

Precise Intentions

Precise intentions are like looking through binoculars. You must know what you are looking for, and in order to spot your target you have to have a general idea where it's located. Even when you are looking straight at your target, in order to see more detail, you need to zoom in. That is what precise intention does, it locates and magnifies that which you want. If you are focused with laser precision on what you want, and are taking action to move towards it, you'll get it. Its sounds easy enough, right? Start your day off intentionally, knowing exactly what you want to have happen, and what you want to achieve.

TOP TIP: I challenge you to start your day by committing to paper your intention to complete certain tasks. Write a list of all of them, and tackle the most difficult one first.

When you complete the most pressing task first you'll experience the rest of the day as a breeze. It will provide you with a sense of accomplishment and the confidence you experience will help ensure a positive outlook. A large or difficult task weighs heavy on our minds, so it is important to get this weight off before handling smaller, easier tasks. If you target smaller, easier tasks first, you may run out of the time and energy needed for the more important ones – those which will get you closer to your goals. The best part of this practice lies in its' ability to help you build the kind of habits which will direct you towards greatness. Let precise intention be a tool which you use daily.

Precise intentions coupled with massive daily action creates supernatural successes. Magnetic forces come to your aid when you know precisely what you want. The right people will be attracted to your life, opportunities will arise, coincidences will abound. Success will begin to show up for you through the power of attraction. I've had many instances of miraculous happenings in my life that bear testament to the power of precise intention. Think of a magnifying glass. The sun can shine relentlessly through it all day with no effect, but if you focus it on a target from a specific angle – fire is created!

Unintentional Fear VS Intentional Love

Fear can feel real even though it is not, and it can have a significant effect on your life. The good news is that you get to decide what role it plays in your life. You can waste your time worrying about all the things that could go wrong, thinking about all the what if's, or you can choose L.O.V.E. Bear with me while I explain.

Fear remains a mental activity, while love manifests as an action. As action is the antidote for fear, love can dispel fear.

F.E.A.R = False Expectation Appearing Real
L.O.V.E = Living Our Vision Every Day

Although we use the acronyms above to remind us about our vision, they also work on our subconscious to make us feel good. Emotional love is certain, optimistic, grateful and abundant. Fear is weak, a thief and a liar. Unlike legitimate danger, fear is not real – it is a thought choice. Everything you want in life is on the other side of fear. It is fear which stops most people from achieving their dreams. Kick fear to the side and choose L.O.V.E. If you dream without fear, you will have the ability to live without limits!

Many unfulfilled dreams result from a fear of failure. Many people choose to focus on what can go wrong, or on the belief that they don't have what it takes. Fear can be as automatic as breathing, and has the potential to affect all of us unintentionally. Fear is not necessary for survival in modern life, as it was for our cavemen ancestors. As unintentional fear is a fact of life, we must be prepared for it when it shows up.

A common example of letting fear govern life is the person who stays in a job they hate for the illusion of security. Another is being guided by a voice that tells you that you may not have what it takes to succeed in a certain field, when in fact you could easily learn the necessary skills.

A really good way to fight fear is to tap into a higher power, in order to cultivate the belief that your dreams will come to pass. I personally choose to believe that there is a Creator; others may have faith in the infinite energy of the universe. Whatever your belief is, it's crucial to tap into a supreme source of energy, and not get caught up in the details of how it will come to you. I am living proof that you can ask a higher source for whatever you desire, and receive it provided it's good for you. Just know that if you don't get something right away, it is because you first require some more growth.

We all have unique talents, but times they go untapped because we lack a belief in ourselves and opt for a safe choice. The reality is that failure is an essential part of growth, so you may as well take a chance and fail at something you love doing, and which you feel passionate about.

At the root of all emotion is either love or fear. Above all else, choose L.O.V.E., and spend time building the life of your dreams. If you love the dreams and goals you are working towards, they will flow to you more easily.

Body language Technique

Although our inner world impacts our outer world, it is possible to alter the way we feel through action. We must be mindful of our body language, as it has a great effect on our mental state. Studies conducted by the Association for Psychological Science at both Columbia and Harvard Universities, looked at the effects of posture and brain function. The study consisted of 42 participants (16 males and 26 females), whose saliva was tested for chemical changes both pre and post-activity. All participants were instructed to stand in either the high-power or low-power pose position, and to hold that pose for one minute.

It was found that those who stood in the high-power pose had increased testosterone levels and decreased cortisol levels. Participants who stood in low-power poses had decreased testosterone levels and increased in cortisol levels. Those in the high power group reported feeling significantly more "powerful" and "in charge". The lesson here is: stand tall, be firm, smile, and avoid low power poses. Adopt positive body language even – or especially – if you don't feel powerful or confident.

INTENTION

"High Power" body language (top row)
vs.
"Low Power" body language (bottom row)

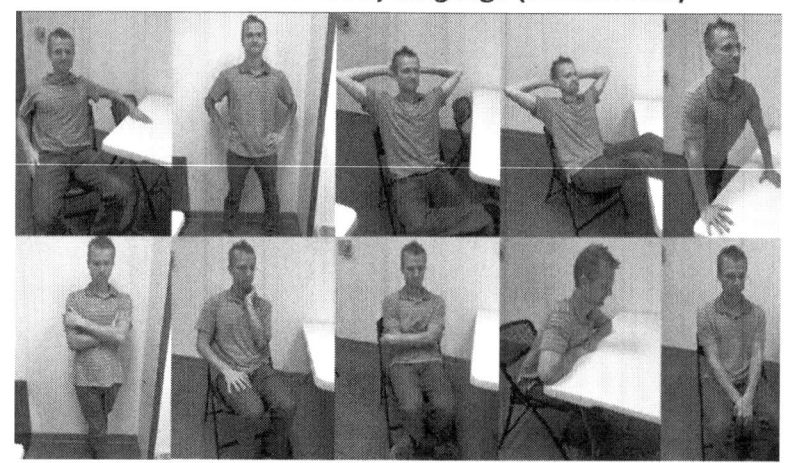

Try adopting the power poses illustrated on the resources page of VisionsToTheTop.com and you'll notice a difference in how you feel. Being more intentional about your posture you will help yourself feel more confident and sure of yourself.

Cortisol is a stress hormone, so the less of it the better. I try to always be aware of how I am standing, and I recommend you do the same. People sense confidence unconsciously through body language, so intentionally adopt power poses throughout the day. In your visualization practice make sure you imagine yourself standing tall in your moment of success.

TOP TIP: Look at the images of high power poses on the resources page of

VisionsToTheTop.com and, with a smile on your face, strike one now. See the difference it makes to the way you feel!

Action Steps

▶ In the morning notice how you wake, Inhale and exhale, Smile think of one thing you are grateful.

▶ Notice your thoughts throughout the day. Remind yourself to keep them positive and powerful aligned with your goals and dreams

▶ Be aware of your body posture. Intentionally practice a couple power poses throughout your day and smile while you do the poses. Notice how doing this changes your mood and feelings.

Chapter 6
Subconscious

Subconscious

"Keep your subconscious mind focused on what you want, and your subconscious mind will unerringly guide you to it."
- Napoleon Hill

    Our thoughts literally create our reality, so whatever you believe to be true becomes your life. Most of our thoughts are not conscious, and the subconscious mind is so powerful that it influences the feelings and actions of everyone. Picture the mind as an iceberg – the conscious mind is the very tip which sticks out of the water, but the subconscious mind is the rest, the 90% lurking beneath in the deep water.

    In order to understand how the subconscious mind works in alignment with your conscious mind let me use a simple analogy of gardening. Below the top level of dirt is a dark rich fertile soil that will grow any seed you place in it. Think of this area as your subconscious mind. What you believe and habitually think are the seeds that you're planting in your most fertile soil. Those thoughts and beliefs will grow quickly and become strong. You've heard the expression "you reap what you sow". If you plant apple seeds you get apple trees. If you plant an avocado seed, you will ultimately grow an avocado tree. This is a law in life. It's the same for our physical reality. If you plant thoughts of abundance, prosperity, and gratitude, you will grow abundance, prosperity and gratitude; and of course the same is true of negative thoughts.

    The conscious mind is like the gardener. As the gardener it's your duty to be aware of what you allow to take root in your garden. Most people have never been taught that we are the creator of our own reality through the thoughts we think. By not fully understanding our role, it is easy to cultivate all kinds of non-helpful thoughts. The wrong seeds take root, and our garden can easily become overgrown with weeds, thanks to the fertile soil of our subconscious mind.

Some people live a life of constant struggle because of the barriers they've dreamt up in their mind. The truth is, the only barriers that exist are the ones you create for yourself. However, even if your mind has been polluted with negativity and false beliefs about money and abundance, it is never too late to change the thoughts in your subconscious mind.

Mind Programing

Just like a computer has programs that run the software, the subconscious mind has been programmed to run you. Your past thoughts and beliefs are the programs that run your daily life, in every way, shape, and form. Sometimes our computers get viruses and don't run smoothly.

Negative thoughts and beliefs are like viruses which prevent a person from being their highest self, and from achieving their greatest potential. In order to be your best self, you need to rewrite your program. This process of change may sound difficult, but with the help of the subconscious mind, it is actually quite simple.

Repetitive Meditation is one way of digging deep into your subconscious mind, and it is possible to intentionally change your subconscious thoughts from this state. I have found that, during meditation, one of the fastest and most effective ways to rewrite self-limiting programs is by visualizing and experiencing my goals as if I am in that moment of time when I am accomplishing them. It's really that simple.

This may seem difficult if you are not familiar with meditation, or if you tried it without success. The truth is, meditation is a practice. Just like learning to ride a bike, you are bound to fall, but if you pick yourself up and try again, you're bound to get it. When practicing to ride a bike you quickly learn that you must keep peddling in order to stay in motion. Likewise, in life, in order to catapult yourself forward and experience quantum leaps of success you will have to keep practicing your meditation. You will notice that some days you will experience an amazing amount of energy after meditating, and other times you won't notice much at all. The key is to keep up a daily practice, intertwining your dreams and goals into your subconscious mind. Eventually, you will redefine who you are and who you dream to be and that will manifest into your reality. I've met the most incredible people who have designed the most wonderful lifestyles imaginable thanks to inner programming through meditation and consciously creating a life of their choosing.

Affirmations and Powerful Questions

Have you ever heard the saying, "The quality of your life is in direct proportion to the quality of questions you ask yourself"?

In 2010, research conducted by Dolores Albarracin, Ibrahim Senay, and Kenji Noguchi at the University of Illinois confirmed the effectiveness of affirmations or "autosuggestion" versus using interrogative self-talk (also known as asking yourself questions). Gurus of self help promote affirmations as one of the key elements for achieving magnetic success, whereas this research revealed the opposite. I like to use a healthy balance of both. The results of this study showed that people who engaged in interrogative self-talk where more effective at solving puzzles after having done so, than those who attempted the same puzzles after engaging in the use of affirmations. In fact, those who asked themselves "Will I solve the puzzles?" did twice as well as those who affirmed to themselves "I will solve the puzzles".

When you ask yourself questions, your brain must respond with answers. Inside the answer is the pathway to your objective. The research shows that when we engage in declarative self-talk "using affirmations" we risk bypassing our motivations.

Interrogative self-talk helps us to elicit our reasons for doing something "our motivation", and reminds people that many of these reasons are internal. Experience has shown me that when I ask powerful questions from a calm state, my subconscious mind provides me with the answers I need to complete the task at hand.

Your best life requires that you to step up the plate equipped with the appropriate questions for any given task. Instead of asking disempowering or doubtful questions, try reframing them as empowering questions.

For example:

A disempowering question would be: Can I hit my goal today?

Reframing this as an empowering question would be: What activities can I do to ensure I hit my goal today?

An example of an affirmation would be: I am determined to become a best-selling author

Reframing this affirmation as interrogative self-talk would be: What specific actions am I committed to doing daily to make sure my book is a best-seller?

You get the message. The idea is to ask yourself empowering questions which prompt you to come up with the best solution. At all costs, you should avoid doubtful, disempowering questions which don't help you move forward.

Imagine for a second that you're on a cruise ship, and your friends ask you to teach a yoga class. (This actually happened to me while I was in the throes of writing this book!) You want everyone to follow your lead, and get as much as possible out of the class. Prior to starting, you could tell yourself "I am the greatest, I am going to deliver an amazing yoga class." This could in fact provide you with an emotional blast of energy. However, the research shows that if you opt to ask yourself, "How can I make this an amazing yoga class", your mind will come up with more valuable, reliable information than affirmations, to help you in the task which lies ahead. Although I was not ready to lead a yoga class it actually went well because I asked myself the right questions.

Your inner self-talk may respond to your challenge by saying, "Yes of course, I'll deliver a healing yoga session. I've been doing yoga for years, and have taught it dozens of times. I will do amazing because…" Repeating affirmations does feel empowering and can definitely help instill confidence in you. The problem is, it will not provide you with the strategies and mental resources you need to actually accomplish your objective.

Should You Turn Your Affirmation into a Question?

There is no doubt that I believe affirmations verbalized in the form of a statement are very powerful tools. However, research shows that adding a few positive questions to your practice makes it optimally effective. You should also be aware that often the answers you are looking for come when you least expect them – perhaps a brilliant idea will come masked as a distant thought. For this reason, always be prepared to write this thought down before it escapes you – either on your phone, or on a notepad which you carry with you for this purpose.

Action Steps

▶ Use affirmations in the morning as a way to trigger excitement about the upcoming day, and to increase your confidence and the belief that you will achieve your goal.

▶ Use Interrogative self-talk when you need to figure out the process for achieving your specific goal. Use this practice throughout the day in order to trigger your mind to find the solution.

Sustainable Affirmations

Personal growth professionals and masters of the Law of Attraction have done a great job of teaching various forms of affirmations. However, because I feel so passionately about the use of affirmations as a vehicle for success, I am proposing a simple way of modifying the traditional use of them - which is sure to propel you towards your goals even faster.

In most cases we are taught to use "I AM" statements in our affirmations. For example, if you want to be a millionaire, you're encouraged to make a statement such as "I am a millionaire", and to repeat it as if it were already true. I would suggest that this sometimes causes inner turmoil because the subconscious mind knows that this statement is not true in this moment. A more powerful way to enlist the help of the subconscious is by modifying your statements to reflect your current situation.

This can be done by adding a few words to your statement in order to be more specific about your goal. Here is the affirmation formula I suggest that top performers use, in order to align themselves with what it is they want to achieve.

How-To: Use the Visions to The Top Affirmations Formula:

Say: "I am dedicated to (insert activity), (insert how often), so that I can (insert goal), by (insert specific date)."

Examples:

1) I am dedicated to making 20 business connections, 3 days a week, so that I grow my business network by December 31st 2016.

2) I am dedicated to writing, 1 hour every day, so that I can finish my book by May 4th 2016.

3) I am dedicated to running, 4 days a week, so that I can hit 365 miles by Dec 31st 2016.

Remember, your subconscious mind will react powerfully to statements which it knows are true, so it is important to not be vague. The above formula works well because it requires you to be precise about your goals: stating what you need to do to achieve them, and setting a deadline for doing so. Using affirmations in this way has been a game changing strategy for me

– I have achieved nearly every goal I have ever set for myself by using it.

Positive Self-Questioning

The more positive questions you ask yourself, the better prepared you will be to receive a promising solution. I like to ask myself these kinds of questions while I'm running on the treadmill, at the end of my meditation, while taking a shower, or drinking a cup of tea or coffee. In fact, several of the ideas in this book came to me while running. When you ask yourself powerful questions be prepared to write down the solutions that appear in the form of an answer. The more powerful positive questions you ask; the more positive solutions will appear. Below are examples of questions that can help you in your process.

1. What activities can I do today and this week that will help bring me closer to becoming the best version of myself?

2. What is the most important thing I need to do right this moment to get me closer to my goal?

3. How can I be the best mom/ husband/ salesperson/ friend?

As you embark on this process, try to remember that intention is like a weight that moves a scale. You can't see it, but if it's set you can feel it. Your set intention will act as a guide, and unseen magnetic forces will pull you towards your vision and dream. It's easy to forget about intention because it's internal. Start paying more attention to it during visualization, and I promise you'll see results. By being intentional during your visualization you plant deep rooted seeds into your subconscious. We will revisit this subject again in the next chapter.

Uncomfortable Beginnings

When I first heard the word programming applied to the workings of the mind, it made me feel uncomfortable. It made me feel as if I was not in control of my own life and thoughts. Little did I realize that my whole life had already been programmed by the words I repeatedly heard from my parents, the television, and songs. The truth is, programming yourself is in fact taking control of your life. The vast majority of people are not privy to this wisdom. However, top performers in every field take charge of programming themselves rather than letting outside influences assume control.

Your subconscious mind is quite happy to keep you acting and thinking in a way that is in line with what you've said and how you've acted in the past. All your well entrenched habits of thought and action -good and bad – are stored in your subconscious mind. It is well acquainted with your comfort zones, and works hard to keep you within them.

Have you ever noticed that any time you learn, or try something new you begin to feel emotionally or physically uncomfortable? This is your subconscious trying to pull you back towards the safety of the known. Your ability to step into new territory is like a muscle which needs to be exercised – it can and will grow stronger if your practice your DAILY VISIONS™ regularly.

The solution to attaining positive change is found in always stretching yourself beyond your comfort zone. The most successful people in life are aware that they are only confined by the walls they have built for themselves. I've heard it said "A comfort zone is a beautiful place, but nothing ever grows there". The level of success you achieve will be in direct proportion to how often you are willing to experience discomfort. If you sincerely want to make changes in your life, then you must change some of your deep rooted beliefs.

By pushing yourself to new limits physically, intellectually, emotionally, and spiritually you will notice a shift in power within yourself. Your inner greatness will begin to shine, as you become more comfortable in your new skin. Success will start to show up in various areas of your life as a result of intentionally empowering your subconscious, and aligning it with your dreams and goals.

The Elephant and the Ant

In his study of both the conscious and unconscious mind, Dr. Lee Pulos found that the conscious mind was capable of processing 2,000 neurons per second, compared to the 2 billion processed by the subconscious during the same second. So, as you're reading this you're probably thinking, "hmmm, this makes sense, I'm enjoying this", while at the same time you might be thinking "I should tell my friend about this", or "I need to meditate more". In other words, there is much thought occurring simultaneously; and with the difference in processing speeds between the conscious and subconscious mind – it is clear that the subconscious is in control!

To conceptualize this visually, imagine that your conscious mind is an ant travelling on the back of an elephant which is your subconscious. If the elephant is travelling South, so is the ant – even if it would prefer to head North!

The bottom line is; we want what's best for ourselves. Consciously we may think "My new year's resolution is to get into shape, and be healthy". The problem is, the subconscious mind might be thinking, "No way, I don't think so, that sounds like a lot of work, that won't be easy!"

Imagine just how effective you would be if your ant and elephant were both headed in the exact same direction?

When you align your elephant and ant then things not only get easier, they become more fun. When they are not in agreement, a bumpy ride is guaranteed. The top performers in any industry have their conscious and subconscious minds aligned. My intention throughout this chapter is to help you understand how to align your conscious with your subconscious in a positive way so that you can achieve whatever you're aiming for.

Meditation Creates Results

I truly believe that Meditation was created as a means by which you can become closer to a higher power. Unfortunately, it is a practice which is overlooked by most people. By silencing your mind, you allow your soul to speak to and be in harmony with the infinite source of energy. My mornings are almost always punctuated by a meditation practice; and when I omit this ritual I feel less happy and fulfilled. Your internal roots grow deeper with meditation, and it allows you to become a stronger version of yourself.

Thoughts are extremely powerful. Everything you see around you is the result of a thought: of something someone dreamt up, believed in, and allowed to take root. If you plant seeds of prosperity and abundance that's exactly what you will grow. The same applies to thoughts of poverty and lacking.

Hopefully you are not the kind of person who is resistant to change, or who refused to believe in something they can't see. In order for you to function at your highest level, you must first believe that it is possible. Meditation will certainly help you feel confident in your ability to succeed. By inserting your thoughts and intentions into your subconscious mind repeated and regularly over a long period of time, you will ultimately create the life you dream. If you continually feed and nourish the fertile garden of your mind with positive input, positive results can't help but result. The key is to be patient with your practice – over time it will strengthen.

This might sound repetitive, but I really want to nail home the concept of "anchored belief". When I nearly cut my hand off I could have easily listened to and believed the doctor when he said that I would never be able to use my hand again. Fortunately for me, I was able to draw on the wisdom I had acquired at various personal growth seminars, and knew that meditation is one of the means by which we can align our inner personal power (the subconscious) with conscious mind.

Meditation is not a one shot deal. In order for alignment to occur one must practice meditation regularly. It is not unlike a strategy used for becoming healthy and fit. In order to increase physical strength and stamina, it is necessary to exercise regularly. Likewise, in order to access the subconscious mind directly, and cultivate mental strength, it will be necessary to adopt a regular meditation practice.

In order to heal my hand, while in meditation I would picture it as strong, I would see it opening and closing, and holding weights. During my practice I would also tap into the feeling of being happy and grateful to have the use of my hand again.

By tapping into feelings and images during meditation, you increase your energetic power, through the ability to manifest these thoughts. These thoughts become an anchor, or trigger. An anchor is a stimulus that helps you to retrieve previously experienced emotions. We are all aware of the way this works in daily life – perhaps we smell a certain perfume and are reminded of someone who wore this particular scent, and are flooded with feelings about that individual. A piece of music might remind of us of a childhood experience, and we are immediately transported back in time. Creating anchors is an important tool, as it allows you to access emotional states of power, and motivation, as you need them.

So next time you meditate, picture your dream or goal with intense focus. Bring that image into your mind and your subconscious will plant that seed in the most fertile soil of your mind, programming plans for you to manifest it. Your subconscious will rewire itself so that you can easily and effortlessly go after that which you seek.

Meditation is such a powerful tool because it acts directly upon the subconscious. The most successful sales people, entrepreneurs, athletes and go-getters use this practice every day. Use it to program your mind for success.

Seeds of Greatness

Manifesting through Meditation should not be limited to money. You should use it to help you achieve all your goals – both long and short term. Many of my friends have told me stories about using meditation to help them find their dream relationships. My wife recalls praying and meditating for a happy and loving relationship. She manifested the ideal of traveling a lot with her marriage partner, of having successful businesses – and that's what she found in me! We are living the life she meditated about.

Dodi Osteen, who is the mother of renowned American televangelist Joel Osteen, was told that she had terminal cancer, and her response was a testament to the power of prayer and meditation. She determined, "If I am going to heal, I have to act like I am healed". She proceeded to line the walls of her house with photos of her younger self, cooked and cleaned, and went about the business of daily living as if everything was normal. She also prayed with strong belief and meditated daily. She continually pictured herself healthy and declared that she was healed. She has never returned to the hospital, and 35 years later is still alive.

Regardless of whether you're looking for health, wealth, happiness, abundance, joy, gratitude, peace, or increased confidence: meditation will help you plant the seeds which will become deeply rooted in your subconscious mind.

Costa Rican Dream

Experiencing lush jungles, endless summers, incredibly tasty foods, and fresh clean air was a dream I had at 20 years of age. After winning a trip to Costa Rica for being a top performer in a sales business, I put owning a gorgeous piece of property in the mountains of this beautiful country on my dream board. I meditated every morning, and visualized getting an amazing deal, and being filled with joy. I could see my land before I owned it. I could feel the emotions of gratitude and happiness before becoming an owner. Within two years, my wife and I went back to Costa Rica and got a "steal of deal" in the Lagunas of Costa Rica. Our land is located at the top of a mountain covered with beautiful yellow mayo trees, shaded and cooled year round, with surreal views of the surrounding landscape. Not only is our land amazing but we have amazing neighbors all around us. I have heard of horror stories of people who go to Costa Rica to buy land. Not us, it was a seamless transaction and we got great deal!

Clues from the Past

Spiritualists, modern scientists, and all of the world's major religions concur that there is a hidden power of intention. Judaism teaches that "prayer without intention is like a body without a soul". Christianity espouses, "You reap what you sow. Islam proclaims, "Everything is based on your intention". Used properly, intention is a very powerful tool. Be mindful of what you intent in your meditation, because you are planting the seeds of your intention deep within the fertile soil of your subconscious. Meditation will ensure that your intentions manifest.

THE FOUR PHASES OF INTENTIONAL MEDITATION

There are so many good reasons for establishing a meditation practice. Studies show that it can help reducing stress levels, lowering blood pressure, strengthening your body's immune system, improve cognitive functioning, increasing productivity and stimulate creative thinking. There seems no good reason for not giving it a try.

So what is meditation anyway? Meditation is time of complete silence, during which you focus on your breath. At first you will find your mind wandering frantically – a phenomenon fondly referred to as "monkey mind" – but the more you practice you will become mentally stronger; your thinking will subside, and you will be able to spend more time just "being". Meditation helps you to calm and empty your mind. I have noticed that meditation works best for me in the morning after prayer, when the world around me is still, calm, and silent. However, you can meditate at any time during the day, as long as you are able to get comfortable, relax, and have access to a place which is devoid of noisy distraction. Whether your meditation practice is 2 minutes or 20 minutes, just focus on what you can do instead of what you can't do. In meditation, always think quality over quantity

How-To: Start Meditating

The meditation practice which I observe and recommend consists of four phases. Each phase can last anywhere from 5 to 20 minutes or longer. When I meditate, I like to set my phone to chime every five minutes to signal moving on to the next phase, but your practice can last as long as you like. I created an audio file just for you that you can play to guide you through meditation at the resources section of VisionsToTheTop.com.

Phase #1 Being – Sit or lie down with your eyes completely covered and closed. Focus on deep breathing (there are any number of breathing techniques available to be learned), and on stillness – not moving at all. This will allow your brain to open to resourcefulness and clarity. Let your brain do the driving – allow your thoughts to flow, and just observe them without judgement. With the help of the breath your brain waves will change and you will transition from a Beta state, to an Alpha state which is characterized by a feeling of calm, and an absence of thinking. Deep relaxation and imagery will occur in the final Theta state.

Phase #2 Active Gratitude – The second phase is a wonderful opportunity for you to remember all the moments in your past which were happy and joyful. Start by looking backwards from the morning, yesterday, last week, a month ago, a year ago, a decade ago. Allow these past moment of gratitude to flow through your mind like a river. These positive memories can include anything from a moment with a loved one, a goal you achieved, a gift you received, a scenic moment in nature, an exciting adventure, a cause for laughter, an accomplishment or achievement. Continue to ride this river of active gratitude as you flow through past moments. This is your "treasure chest" of past memories.

In this Phase, you are priming the mind with belief and confidence. Confidence is real because it is linked to actual evidence. By triggering past experiences of gratitude and victory you are opening a flow of confidence, which will be used in the next phase.

Phase #3 Primed and Ready – Phase 3 is where you play "what if" with a positive spin.

Imagine your mind working things out the way you'd like them to be. Avoid all negative takes on any situation. Keep your thought pattern only positive. Focus on the goals and dreams that you intend for the future. This creates strong vibrations within you, because you are already primed with the confidence of past successes.

Sometimes people make the mistake to try to jump right into visualization and meditation when they're not feeling good or not happy. It is a mistake to meditate when your feelings are all over the place. You cannot create a beautiful vision if you're in a place of mental resistance. Your vibrations have to be aligned. That is why it is crucial to practice Phase 2 "Active Gratitude" before Phase 3 "Primed and Ready". With confidence flowing through you, you are liable to think, "Yeah I achieved this and that before, so this new idea is definitely attainable".

Practicing these phases in order will make it easier to see yourself on the stage winning the award, or to imagine yourself with that amazing person, or see yourself in that dream home. Your brain has a hard time disbelieving your visions, because you'll have filled it with multiple examples of positive past experiences.

Phase #4 Accepting – You will finish up your meditation practice sitting or lying in the position you started in. This final phase is all about acceptance. You will be feeling relaxed and amazing because your cortisol levels have plummeted, and your brain is pumping out dopamine and serotonin - flooding your bloodstream and making you feel like you're on cloud nine. Now you get the chance to experience the benefits which your brain is capable of producing.

Sometimes you get great ideas during the accepting phase of your meditation practice. The Daily V.I.S.I.O.N.S idea came to me during phase 4 of practice. I asked myself if there was something I had been doing for years that I could share with the world in order to make a positive difference. The answers to your most important questions are within you – you just need some time and space to quiet the mind, and the answer will come.

I've heard so many incredible stories from people of every walk of life, about the incredible ideas that have sprung forth during meditation. Many people go into meditation with the intention of seeking an answer to a specific question. The Accepting phase opens the door which allows the Creator or Universe, to provide that answer you're seeking.

After you've completed all four stages, you will feel calm and collected. Now open your eyes and start your day!

Chapter 7
Inspiration

Inspiration

A working definition of inspiration is: a force that makes someone want to achieve something or makes them want to create something or an influence that inspires someone.

Wouldn't it be awesome to wake up every day of your life and feel like you're were on holiday? To feel super fired up when you wake up in the morning before your alarm? Feeling like this is possible, if you are aligned with your goals, dreams and purpose in life. Image what it would be like to be the one standing on stage in the spotlight, instead of being a spectator and watching life from a distance.

When you're inspired, you get the chance to meet life head on and make things happen instead of standing on the sidelines and seeing it pass you by. In this section I will relate stories from my experiences and those of others, which will hopefully inspire you to pursue your best life ever.

Now that you're aware of the power of your subconscious mind and how important it is to align it with your conscious mind, consider putting reminders in different places throughout your house to act as triggers.

TOP TIP - Start writing your largest and most exciting goal in erasable marker on the bathroom mirror. Be sure to include a deadline – this will light a fire under you and will help to ensure that you take the necessary actions.

Viewing your goal regularly will trigger your subconscious and activate the power of visualization. All that remains is the need for a firm belief in the idea that you'll achieve that goal, and taking the daily action necessary to move you towards it. Some people get creative with colored sticky notes and place them by light switches in their home. Others write their goals in affirmation form and put them somewhere they'll be sure to see every day. My friend Julian in New Orleans has his affirmations posted on the door to his room so he sees them every time he leaves and enters. Some people prefer a digital option, for them I recommend using the Evernote App. I use the dry eraser method because it enables me to easily edit once I achieve a goal and want to create a new one.

A number of business people I know use this activity along with visualization as a way to propel them towards their goals. A friend in Austin, Josh, uses this technique and is repeatedly the #1 distributor for his company. He's sold millions of dollars in products, has a thriving coaching business, a booming marketing company, and very fulfilling marriage. He attributes his success to being tapped into his goals and dreams, and having a laser-like focus when it comes to achieving them.

People often ask me, "How do you stay so inspired?". It's actually quite simple. The highest version of ourselves is hard-wired to achieve, create, and pursue greatness. The secret is knowing exactly what your dreams are and having a plan for achieving them within a certain timeframe. I will have more to say on this subject in the section on NonNegotiable. At the root of all success there must be the belief that you can achieve your goals, the knowledge of precisely what you want, and a plan of action which you execute daily.

When you are tapped into your dreams, inspiration flows through you like caffeine. This alignment gives you a sense of excitement, passion, and personal power. Inspiration allows us to complete the difficult tasks, to show up, and put in the extra hours. Energy flows where focus goes. Just be careful to not run out of gas. There are many internal and external variables that help to keep your energy level high and your gas tank full of inspiration. Here are some suggestions:

INSPIRATION TOOL KIT

Internal	External
Prayer	A vision board
Meditation	A vacation
Visualization	A great book
Positive thoughts	The words you say
Belief in self	Working out
	The people in your life
	A Melody, Ted talk, pod cast

People often say inspiration doesn't last – well, neither does having fresh smelling breath, that's why we need to brush our teeth daily! How you choose to spend your time will have a great impact on your inspiration levels. Different activities produce different energy levels, and there are even healthy and unhealthy ways to spend down time. My inspiration comes from doing good, making moral decisions, and living by the golden rule of treating others the way I would like to be treated.

The Six Human Needs: Why we do what we do

Before I jump into this incredibly important section, I want to give credit where it is due. The life changing information I am about to impart exists thanks to the work of human needs psychologist Chloe Madanes, and became popularized by motivational speaker Tony Robbins.

There is a wealth of information available on this subject, so I will only touch on it briefly and elaborate on a few of the points which I know will help you become a better version of yourself. We all have the following needs, each of us deciding which ones to nurture in our lives.

THE SIX HUMAN NEEDS

    1. Certainty - The need for security, stability, and reliability.

    2. Variety/Uncertainty - The need for challenge, change, and stimulation.

    3. Significance - The need to feel valued, acknowledged, and recognized.

    4. Love and connection - The need to feel love and give love, and feel connection with other people.

    5. Growth - The need to improve ourselves and personally develop - also known as personal growth both in character and spirit.

    6. Contribution - The need to help others, give, and make a difference.

Of the 6 human needs, everyone unconsciously chooses to focus on 2 of them at the expense of the others. These become our driving forces, informing all that we do. If a person is driven by growth and contribution, they will inevitably be full of gratitude, and feel content and fulfilled. All other needs will flow effortlessly through their life.

Unfortunately, the vast majority of people focus on certainty and significance, and this can render suffering and a sense of discontent. In addition, there are many unhealthy ways in which the needs for certainty and significance can be filled, including substance abuse, eating disorders, and controlling behavior. Moreover, acting out of a need for certainty and significance often results in anger and depression.

When you start on a journey of personal growth, it is important to be aware of the "automatic" thoughts which govern your behavior. Regardless of whether you identify yourself as a student, parent, or business person, there are unseen emotional triggers which underpin your actions. Awareness of these triggers is the first step towards changing your behavioral patterns. Early on in my journey, I realized that I had anger issues which I was able to overcome when I came to know what situations triggered this emotion. This was an important turning point in my life, which enabled me to accept my past and present in order to have an inspired future.

I recommend that you spend more time learning about the Six Human Needs. Doing so will help you understand how others are reacting to you, and will help you lead whatever group or organization you are associated with.

How-To: Focus on Growth and Contribution

> *"If you run your life or organization with a focus on growth and contribution, the right people show up, the right situations occur, and favorable things begin to happen."*
>
> –Justin Ledford

In order to make **growth** a priority in your life, try focusing on the following courses of action:

1. Be Accepting – Accept yourself just as you are today, in every area of your life.

Whether good or bad, know that where you are today is exactly where you need to be.

2. Embrace Learning – Access personal growth tools which include good books, audiotapes, podcasts, Ted Talks, or a personal coach. Try watching inspirational documentaries instead of mainstream TV.

3. Network – Expand your social circle to include people who you want to emulate – either because they are more successful than you, or because they are doing something you want to do.

4. Stretch your brain – Broaden your understanding of the world and your place in it. Challenging your beliefs will help you grow.

5. Travel – Take the opportunity to see how others live, even if it's only in your own city.

In order to make **contribution** a priority in your life, try focusing on the following courses of action:

1. Give – There are so many organizations which can benefit from charitable donations of money, or items which you no longer have a use for.

2. Volunteer – A gift of time can consist of feeding the less fortunate at a soup kitchen, coaching a kid's sports team, or volunteering for any number of jobs at a hospital, school, or place of worship.

3. Teach – Always look for opportunities to impart what you know to those who will listen.

4. Recycle – Live an environmentally friendly life in which recycling is part of your lifestyle. Or try to refrain from using single use plastics.

The Importance of Living with Integrity

Integrity is the quality of being honest, and of living a life guided by strong moral principles. You can achieve material success in any way you like, but if you live your life without integrity it is, in my opinion, a failure. There is no point in attaining material abundance, if you lose yourself in the process.

I have met many "successful" people who have compromised themselves in an effort to rise to the top. Lying, cheating, backstabbing, and a lack of honor are characteristics of people who are living in a lower state of consciousness. Those who are willing to cut corners are not the right people to have in your circle. You save time when you do things right the first time, and less mental energy is consumed when you live an honest life.

When a light is turned on in a dark room the light penetrates the darkness. The same is true in our lives. When we act in accordance with our highest self, our inner light beams brightly, simplifying our path and lighting the way for those around us. Always remember that what goes around comes around, so it is in your own best interest to treat others well.

If it seems as if your life is not progressing in the way you want, and you find yourself constantly in conflictual situations – maybe there is something in your character that can be improved upon. Take it as a sign that you need to change the needs which you are focusing on.

Sharing is Contagious

I believe that deep within every human being is the need to contribute. This can manifest as those around you wanting to help, if you understand how this principle works.

I first noticed this while selling at various trade shows, and observing what it was that inspired people to want to spend their money with me. I found that people were more willing to buy what I had to offer if I informed them of my sales goal, telling them why it was important for me, and letting them know what I stood to win if I achieved it. Building a rapport with people in this way seemed to entice them to want to buy into my vision. This is in fact a winning sales technique, and I call it The Persuasion Equation. It works as follows:

THE PERSUASION EQUATION

"In business as in life you don't get what you deserve, you get what you negotiate"
– Chester Karrass

+ Share your goal sincerely.
+ Quickly mention your deadline and the prize you hope to win
+ Offer the person an incentive or bonus for helping you
= A closed deal and money in the bank

This strategy can help you in business, but playing to people's desire to help can also help make your dealings with family and friends run more smoothly.

You Have Only Two Choices

You have only two choices in life: to either be inspired or discouraged by the events in your life. When I arrived home after slicing through my hand and being told I could have died from loss of blood, I was seeped in negativity for the first few days, unable to see the light at the end of the tunnel. My focus became very narrow, because I was concerned with my ability to find significance and certainty within this new reality. This caused me to question, "Why me", and to dwell on the pain.

I quickly realized that this choice of action would get me nowhere. Complaining and whining only made me feel miserable. Thankfully I didn't get too attached to feeling this way. I quickly found a way to use this experience as the inspiration to do great things, and I began to focus on action which was in my realm of control.

I speak from experience when I say life is much more fulfilling and fun when you opt for an inspired existence.

Develop a No Excuses Mentality

Another way in which the need for certainty and significance manifests is in an attitude of negativity embodied in excuses. Personally, I am not wired to listen to excuses, hearing someone explain why they didn't get something done, or how something didn't go their way saps my energy and doesn't help them to move forward.

Instead of making excuses, choose growth and work at finding solutions and encourage the same in those around you. The next time someone comes to you with an excuse or complaint, I recommend saying something such as, "I understand what you're going through. What is something you can do to help yourself get through it?"

Being considerate is important when dealing with people, and you can contribute to another's well-being by listening and helping them find a solution. Buying into someone's negativity is not only unhelpful, it can also derail you – preventing you from progressing towards your goal. We all have to accept the fact that some people are stuck in a way of being that is negative. Have your radar out for people who love to complain and walk a wide circle around them!

Top performers don't make excuses. They show up with results, and if they can't figure something out on their own, they find someone who can, one who can do it for them or learn how to do it themselves. Cultivate a "no excuses" mentality, and notice the liberation you feel from meeting life head on.

Observe the Five Minute Rule

When something over which you have no control goes wrong in your business or personal life, you always have a choice about how to react. There is little point in getting upset if it was something you could not control. I once had a manager who taught me a valuable strategy to use in situations like this, and I use it to this day. I call it the "Five Minute Rule".

When you boil water in a tea kettle, steam escapes from the built up pressure. The same thing happens to you when you become upset about something. Allowing yourself five minutes to moan, complain, whine, stomp your feet, or anything else which allows your "steam" to escape is healthy. Anything beyond five minutes adds no further value, and can in fact be unhealthy.

How to: Get & Stay Inspired

1) Place positive reminders throughout your home

2) Make personal growth and contribution your driving forces

3) Use the Persuasion Equation, and share your excitement about things with others

4) Take responsibility for your own life by adapting a "No Excuses" approach

5) Let go of things over which you have no control by using the "Five Minute Rule"

Chapter 8
Opportunity

Opportunity

"If someone offers you an amazing opportunity and you're not sure you can do it, say yes – then learn how to do it later"
                                        - Richard Branson

A working definition of opportunity is: A set of circumstances that makes it possible to attain a goal.

Opportunity is everywhere. This is especially true if you live in a First World country. The greatest opportunities occur when you push beyond your comfort zone. Take this example of a poor man living in the Middle East, who noticed an opportunity and ran with it. It is every Muslim's obligation to undertake the annual pilgrimage to Mecca at least once in their lifetime. The journey requires that they bring something to carry their goods in. He noticed that cardboard boxes were routinely discarded, and had the idea to claim them for resale to pilgrims in need at a minimal cost. With millions of people making the journey to Mecca each year, over time this trash translated into millions of dollars. If someone of limited means can create a million-dollar enterprise out of cardboard boxes, don't you think you can find ways to create opportunity in your life?

The Right Mindset to Be Open to Opportunity

There was a study in which they used participants with different belief systems in order to investigate the role of mindset in recognizing opportunity.

One participant had a positive attitude which led them to report feeling "blessed", thinking that "things come easy to them", and believing that "life is good no matter what". The other subject reported feeling that they were "always just getting by", were "doing ok", believing that "nothing ever comes easy". Each participant was given money for a coffee and were instructed to go into a busy Starbucks and buy a cup.

The researchers had placed a $20 bill in plain view on the floor inside the coffee shop, and waited to see how the participant would react. The first participant entered the Starbucks, immediately spotted the $20 bill, asked of those around him "did anyone drop this", then walked up to the counter where he ordered a latte and had a pleasant conversation with the Barista. At the sugar counter he struck up a conversation with a businessman who complimented him on his cheerful manner with the server. He said he was a regular at that Starbucks and rarely noticed such congeniality. In the conversation which ensued, the subject found out that this man was a venture capitalist, something which he had been interested in for some time. Remarkably, they went on to create a successful business together.

The second participant did not fare so well. She walked into the coffee shop carrying herself poorly, and stepping right over the $20 bill. With little fanfare she ordered a coffee, had limited conversation, and left without lifting her eyes from the safety of her phone.

The difference in outcome for the two participants in this study is not the result of coincidence. While not everyone ends up with the type of result that the first participant experienced, having a positive attitude has everything to do with seeing and capitalizing on the opportunities which present themselves in your life.

Although I have a "can do" attitude it doesn't come automatically and it's something

I still work on to this day. I notice that when I have a "can do" attitude in life doors open for me, and things seem to come easy. How many opportunities are you missing out on every day by not being open and engaging with others?

TOP TIP: Post messages in your home which will help to program your subconscious mind for greatness. Here are a few suggestions:
- I can do this
- I am blessed
- Wonderful opportunities always come to me
- Everything comes to me easily
- Life is amazing

An Abundance Mentality vs A Scarcity mentality

"Abundance is not something we acquire. It is something we tune into"
— Wayne Dyer

Why do some people seem to have everything they want in life, and appear happy and optimistic? The truth is, their positive attitude has the power to attract abundance into their lives. You too can align yourself with abundance. Your ability to adapt a positive attitude is like a muscle which will become stronger the more you foster it.

The choice to create an abundant life is available to everyone. By practicing meditation, visualization, and positive speech your thought pattern will begin to form into a mindset of abundance. Intentionally tapping into your dreams and goals will produce a magnetic frequency. However, a belief has absolutely no power of attraction if you don't think it will come true.

To illustrate the power to attract abundance, consider what my wife and I encounter in the operation of our construction company. When we launch a group of salespeople out into the field for the first time, we are actually able to observe the alignment of a positive attitude with success.

The task of our sales force is to knock on doors in neighborhoods, they are instructed to inform homeowners that they can get work done to their home.

Every Tuesday we meet with the newly launched team. Regardless of having worked the same neighborhood, they report one of two kinds of experience. Those who come back with contracts make comments such as "I knew I would hit my goal", or "It was tough, but I was committed". Those who were less successful invariably quit, or report back with excuses such as "nobody was home", "nobody had money", or "there was too much competition in the neighborhood".

Do you have a mentality of abundance or scarcity? Do the thoughts that flow through your mind, or the words that come out of your mouth set you up for greatness, or hold you back from achieving your full potential?

Opportunity is Everywhere You Look

> *"Fortune favors the bold."*
> **-Latin Proverb**

In order to catch fish, you have to have bait. To be successful at catching bait, you have to cast your net where there is the most activity in the water. If you throw it randomly you may catch a few minnows, but if you toss it into heavily populated waters, you will be assured of having enough bait for the entire day.

The same principle applies to the running of your life and business. Your courage is your net. If you half-heartedly cast it, you may come up with a few prospects. If you are bold enough to throw it out there with passion and an expectation of success, you will have more prospects than you know what to do with. Just know that opportunity is everywhere and it has no slow season - for the person with the right mindset, there will be no days off.

Opportunity Favors The RIGHT Productivity

When I first started out as an entrepreneur I wasn't used to setting my own schedule. I quickly learned that whether you earn your living from selling, creating, writing, coaching, speaking, or even working for someone else you owe it to yourself to make the best use of your time, and structure your day in way that facilitates the best possible outcomes.

The biggest mistake which most people make is mistaking busy work for being productive. While checking your emails, and listening to voicemails are important, they are usually not activities which will directly generate income. Try to think of your day as a bucket. If you fill it with pebbles and sand (emails and unscheduled tasks), there will be no room left for the big rocks (productive tasks). Top performers know to get the most productive task done first and later in the day do the busy task.

BIG

TASK
FIRST

It is extremely important that you learn to prioritize, and this means attending to your most important tasks first. You should always have a good idea what your most important tasks are. As an entrepreneur, these are anything which will generate business. Steven Covey, the author of the award winning book "The 7 Habits of Highly Effective People" recommends first tackling the one or two tasks which have the potential to move your business forward. Doing so not only allows you to attack them at the start of the day when your energy is at its' highest, but it will allow you to start the day with a true sense of accomplishment. Win the morning, and you'll win your day!

That said, I have found certain times of day work better with certain tasks than others. For example, in sales I find that calling prospects from 8-10 am and again from 7-9 pm is more effective than calling throughout the day. In a business that requires sales people to go door to door weekends and afternoons are best because that's when people are usually home.

It's easy to find amazing examples of productivity in nature, and in doing so to see the infinite wisdom created in all aspects of life. Take for example the humble bee. Bees are entirely focused on productive action. Their objective is to collect nectar juice to bring back to the hive for the purpose of making honey. They understand the need to do what is most important for everybody in their community to thrive, and work as a team. They have courage to seek bounty every day, without the fear of being eaten. Like the top performers in any enterprise, they courageously embrace the opportunity to succeed.

TWO TASK CHALLENGE

What are the two biggest tasks you need to achieve each morning, in order to move closer to your goal?

Be Prepared

> *"The Successful warrior is the average man, with laser-like focus"*
> – Bruce Lee

Sailing a boat requires total focus. At each moment you have to be intentional in terms of your direction, otherwise you will coast along aimlessly – never reaching your destination. The same applies to every situation in life and business, you can choose to be focused and active, or tuned out. With active intention that is directed towards opportunity, you can't help but feel the pull of success. It is important to be prepared in order to receive opportunities.

Imagine for a second that you are thrust onto an ancient battlefield. If you were put in this situation you'd want to be as prepared as possible equipping yourself with knives and swords. Your main focus would be to protect yourself, stay alive, be efficient with your energy use, and to assist your comrades in battle. In the day to day battles of life, you also need to show up prepared. When you have a mindset that allows you to see opportunities and your intention is set towards your goal there is an energy that will draw you to it.

Entertain Yourself To Success

> *"We aren't in an information age, we are in an entertainment age"*
> – Tony Robbins

There are people in your life that have achieved or are achieving exactly what you want. Doesn't it make sense to model their success? These people have literally failed their way to the top, they've made the mistake, figured out what works best, systematized it, and are now running with a strategy that works. The advice I followed and that which I offer to you is that you emulate someone you admire in order to receive the kind of results you're looking for. Follow the wisdom which comes from their experience, no matter what area of your life you wish to improve upon. Whether you want to" Become a Better Spouse", or learn "How to write a book", or "How to practice meditation", there is no shortage of information readily available to you.

While driving or working out you should consider listening to a podcast, or an inspirational Ted talk - something which allows you to grow intellectually, instead of listening to music. Maybe you don't have somebody in your immediate circle who can inspire you to be your best self, but my buddies over at youtube have you covered. Instead of always seeking to be entertained, seek to be learning and your efforts will be cut in half.

However, always remember that knowledge is only power if it is applied. Anything you want can be achieved as long as you're willing to learn the skills needed to reach your objective.

Determine Best Skills and Use Them Accordingly

In order to rise to the top in business, it is important to know exactly what your strengths are and focus your efforts here. Most people make the mistake of spending the lion's share of their time improving their weaknesses, and this is a faulty strategy.

Focusing on things which you are not particularly good fosters negativity. It is much more efficient to delegate anything which falls outside of your skill base. For example, I used to work all day and then come home and spend hours processing thousands of dollars-worth of orders until 11 or 12 pm. Finally, I hired a specialized assistant to our office who was prepared to take on the task. This freed up the time for me to pursue the things I love and am good at, like writing this book, and gardening.

The lists below represent some of my strengths and weaknesses, and I suggest you use them as a guide for creating your own.

My Strengths	Areas to Improve or Delegate
Interacting with customers	Responding to emails
Speaking in crowds	Following up
Networking	Making phone calls
Quickly building a solid rapport	Be patient
Learning from top performers	Marketing
Training people	Data entry

Ask yourself what you are best at and what areas are in need of improvement. What are your strengths? What do you enjoy doing?

This activity has helped my coaching clients see tremendous growth in their businesses.

Focusing your limited time on things which you're not great at and which you don't like makes no sense. Know your strengths and weakness and learn how to delegate.

Work smart and hard and you will feel the universe supporting your efforts by delivering opportunities to you.

Chapter 9
Non-Negotiables

Non-Negotiables

"Make your dreams as non-negotiable as the air you breathe"
- Justin Ledford

In order to live up to our highest potential we need to inject certain rituals into our daily routine. These are things which must be practiced regularly, and which lay the foundation for greatness. These are what I call the non-negotiables, and the next few pages will outline exactly what they are.

Non-Negotiable Dream Management

After interviewing hundreds of top performers in all walks of life it became clear to me what foundational habits characterize the daily lives of highly successful people, the results were obvious. The non-negotiable practices of those at the top help to instill strength, courage, focus, and "I can do this" type of attitude. With our coaching clients at Top Success Coaching we have them commit to what we call non-negotiables.

From one of my favorite books, "The Dream Manager" by Mathew Kelly I got the message that it is essential to live your dreams instead of just dreaming and hoping that they will come true. In order to live the best version of yourself while creating the life of your dreams, you have to know exactly what it is that you want in life. Assessing exactly what your dreams are and having them written down on one page which you can refer to regularly is key. In my calendar we make dreams list for 1 year and we make Dream list for 5 years down the road. Living life by design starts here. If you could have life your way, how would you spend your days and nights?

There are specific areas of your life that will need to be targeted if you want to have a life which is happy, fulfilling, and full of gratitude. These can be classified as: Intellectual, Physical, Spiritual, Emotional, Financial, Material, Adventure, Professional, Creative, Character, Psychological, and Legacy.

I keep my dream list visible in my daily calendar. Use my dream list as a template for creating your own list. Have you thought to yourself, "I would love to write a book", or, "I would love to go to (insert your dream destination)", or, "I would love to lose 30 pounds", or, "It would be so awesome to save 20k this year". Instead of saying "I would" or "I wish", together let's make it our intention from now on to say "I will (insert dream)".

As I said earlier, my dreams list is written down on the last page of my daily calendar for easy reference and then these exact dreams are then put on the vision board. You may want to consider printing your list and placing it wherever works best for you. To print a premade handout go to www.VisionsToTheTop.com in the resources section and it is available for download. I also block off periods of time in which to chip away at my dreams. Since I started this practice, I have become more joyful, healthier, and my relationships are flourishing. My spirit is fulfilled, my mind is stronger, and my income has increased tremendously! Aren't these things which you want for your life?

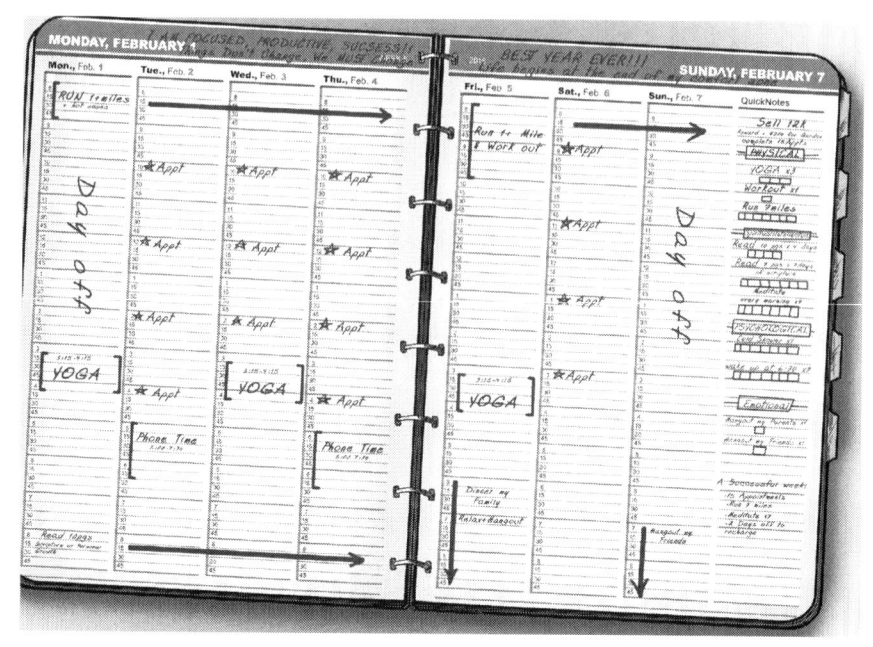

TOP TIP: Spend 1 hour on Sunday afternoon in the window of 6-11pm to plan out your ideal week. Remember to use your dream list and intertwine your dreams into your everyday calendar. Our goal is life by design not default!

This is such a powerful task, and so simple!

ACTION STEPS

▶ Set aside 30-45 minutes when you can be undisturbed, and focus your energy on this activity of writing your dreams list.

▶ Get your planner out, or a piece a paper, or your journal. I highly recommend you hand write your dreams list instead of typing them out.

▶ Don't spend much time thinking - just write whatever dreams you aspire to achieve down on paper.

Next, schedule some time to work on a couple of your dreams. My mentor Hal Elrod author of The Miracle Morning, once taught me the simplest way of getting stuff done is by adhering to the "Butt in chair" rule – aligning specific tasks with specific blocks of time. This is the only way to ensure that spending time working on your dreams becomes a habit. When you make your non-negotiables a priority, you will begin to move in the direction of your dreams.

How do you feel now that you filled out your dream list in your calendar? Consider sharing your calendar with other Visionaries on the private Facebook community at <u>www.VTTTVisionaries.com</u>

> *"The two most important days of your life: Are the day you were born, and the day you find out why"*
>
> **- Mark Twain**

Chapter 10
Sacrifice

Sacrifice

"Don't wish it was it was easier, wish you were better. Don't wish for less challenges, wish for more wisdom."

– Jim Rohn

A working definition of sacrifice is: an act of giving up something valued for the sake of something else regarded as more important or worthy. In order for you to have everything you want, and to become the person you dream of being, there will definitely have to be sacrifices.

You are responsible for the way your life looks, if you're unhappy you will need to make changes. The world is in desperate need of people who are self-sufficient, and who are willing to roll up their sleeves in an effort to better themselves. In an effort to do so, it will be necessary to sacrifice the little things now, so that later you can have the big things you always wanted. Jerry Rice once said, "Today I will do what others won't, so tomorrow I can do what others can't."

The Marshmallow Experiment

To illustrate how making little sacrifices can pay off, let me tell you about my favorite study of delayed gratification, which was conducted in the 1960's.

Hundreds of children were brought one by one into a room where they were offered a deal. They were given a marshmallow and told that if they didn't eat it over the course of the next 15 minutes, they would be rewarded with a second marshmallow. In other words, they could eat one treat now, or two later.

The video footage of these kids struggling to not eat the marshmallow is hilarious. Some resorted to petting the marshmallow, others turned to face the other direction, while still others jumped up and down trying to avoid eye contact with the treat. Some ate it right away and some restrained their desires the whole time.

Now let's talk about how this study applies to you. The children who participated in this study were tracked for over 40 years, and it was found that the ones who had been able to delay gratification were more financially successful, smarter, heathier, and less stressed than those who had eaten the first marshmallow.

Are there areas of your life in which you could practice delayed gratification? Remember that little changes can make big differences. Do you need to start going to bed earlier so you can wake up earlier? Can you commit to spending less time in front of the TV? Would you be able to spend less money on random stuff you really don't need, or exercise more frequently? Choose an area in which you can afford to sacrifice. Begin to focus on it, and see what happens.

Taking Action – Laying the bricks

I spoke about building an intentional pathway to success in the section on Visualization. Remember, visualization alone will not help us realize our dreams. We cannot have good intentions and a solid visualization practice and then just sit on the couch with our finger in our belly button. We have to get up and get things done. Taking action is the laying of bricks in your pathway, and it will involve sacrifice.

Action without vision is a nightmare, but having a vision which is not acted upon is little more than a daydream. The distance between your dreams and reality is called action.

In order to rise to the top, you will need to put your money where your mouth is. If you have a dream of starting a business, or building a garden, writing a book, being an amazing mother/father or any other dream for that matter, put it in your daily calendar, and earmark some time to start conquering it. Each time you swing an ax at a log you get that much closer to chopping through it. This is the same with dreams. You need to chip away at them with daily action.

Little Habits Change Your Life

Regardless of where you are in your journey of life it is always possible to do better, to have a more fulfilling life. Sacrifice is giving up something good for something better. Changing the little things in life can have a big impact on ourselves, our families, and society at large.

It's been said that how you do anything is how you do everything. So if every day you shut off your alarm so that you can snooze a little longer, spend too much on non-important items, or watch too much TV, changing small behaviors in these areas can have a large impact on the direction your life takes you.

A Habit to Lead to Riches

> *"Save money and money will save you"*
> **– Jamaican Proverb**

Some people say money doesn't buy happiness and I agree, but it sure makes life easier. It is a tool that can be used to help you achieve greatness. Regardless of your personal finances, there is one principle which applies across the board, and which I unfortunately learned the hard way.

Over the course of eight successful years selling products, I managed to make a lot of money. During this time, I was healthy, wealthy, but not wise! I spent so much of my money on stuff – things I didn't need to impress people that did not really matter. I am going to share with you what I know and do now.

The key to wealth is paying yourself first – saving money every paycheck, or however your money is delivered to you – and placing this money in an account which you don't touch. When you can't see it, you won't spend it. Live now how others won't, so later you can live like others can't. This is the entrepreneur's mantra.

A great book to read on building wealth is "The Secrets of the Millionaire Mind" by T Harv Eker. One powerful and simple suggestion in the book is that every time you receive money you divide it into different buckets before spending a dime. Below is a quick example of what you would do with $1000.

Bucket 1: 55% goes to Necessities = $550
Bucket 2: 10% goes to WBA (Wealth Building account) = $100
Bucket 3: 10% goes to GRO (Personal Growth Account) = $100
Bucket 4: 10% goes to LTSS (long term savings spending) = $100
Bucket 5: 10% goes to PLAY (Play account) = $100
Bucket 6: 5% is to GIVE away to less fortunate = $50

Necessities are exactly what you might imagine: food, shelter, gas, cell phone, electricity. A Wealth Building Account is crucial for long term wealth. This money is invested into a business for profit: a 401k, 403b stock market, IRA, or a Roth IRA. Look for good growth funds that have a long track record of success that produce 10% or better over a 20-year period. The money that is invested here won't be touched for many years, so it has a chance to compound – allowing you to retire wealthy.

The money in a GRO is invested in yourself: on books, seminars, a personal life coach, anything that allows you to grow intellectually or spiritually. Long term saving spending is money accumulated for the purchase of a vehicle, TV, or any item you would like to buy down the road. Play money is spent on entertainment: concerts, vacations, or anything else you deem as being fun. Your Give account is for charitable donations – try it and see for yourself that the more give, the more you will receive. Don't give money to get more money, give money sincerely from your heart and you'll notice what goes around comes around.

Even if you make a really decent income, if you don't know how to manage your money you will never accumulate wealth.

Spend Mindlessly or Consciously – It's Your Choice

What can you cut out of your monthly spending? Do you go out to eat or buy a coffee at Starbucks every day? When's the last time you evaluated your monthly expenses? What are services that you are not using but getting charged for every month because you haven't yet cancelled them? By mindlessly spending money on stuff we don't need we are wasting money. Decide what truly makes you happy and spend your money on this instead. Always remember to be wise how you spend your money, even more importantly always pay yourself first by putting money away in your wealth building account.

Here are a few things consider:

If you're between 16 and 20 years of age, don't be in a rush to move out on your own if you don't have to. Instead invest in an IRA, or a Roth IRA, and save for the down payment on a house.

If you're between 21 and 30 years of age, stop buying stuff you don't need to impress people who really don't care about you. Save that money and put it in a retirement fund that will increase every year, and by the time you're 65 you'll be well off. I'm light years ahead of my peers because I sacrifice to saving and stick to a budget. If you're between 30 and 60 years of age, make sure you take care of your health. Also realize that it is never too late to start living the life of your dreams. A few bodily aches and pains can be surmounted by regular exercise, yoga, meditation and visualization techniques. Pursue inner and outer excellence.

To underscore the importance of money management, let me give you an example of a person with an average income of $30,000 a year who decides to use the wealth buckets approach for 20 years, investing only 10% of their income, or $3,000 a year.

This person decides to pack a lunch and make their own coffee at home in order to save $12.50 a day. Multiple this by 5 days a week, and you come up with $62.50 a week. Multiple this by 4 weeks and it amounts to $250 a month. Multiple it one last time by 12 months, and this person arrives at their goal of $3000. Do you realize how much that would increase your WBA (Wealth Building Account) 20 years later at only 10% return?

$3000 a year for 20 years will equal $60,000 invested! That $60,000 invested over the course of 20 years increases to $189,007.48. Once I understood how this concept worked, I started packing my lunch almost every day and bought my own cappuccino machine! I was a little concerned when I first signed up for an automatic 10% deduction from my paycheck, but my portfolio has grown handsomely since I've started and yours can to! Now my only regret is that I didn't start earlier.

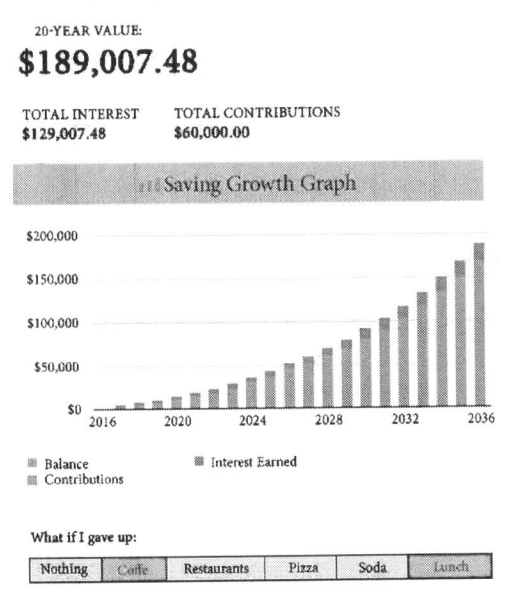

20-YEAR VALUE:
$189,007.48

TOTAL INTEREST: $129,007.48
TOTAL CONTRIBUTIONS: $60,000.00

Saving Growth Graph

- Balance
- Contributions
- Interest Earned

What if I gave up: Nothing | Coffe | Restaurants | Pizza | Soda | Lunch

The numbers are even more staggering for a person making $100,000 a year investing only 10% a year equaling $10,000 x 20 years equals $200,000 invested. That $200,000 invested over the course of 20 years increases to $630,022.47. Not too shabby just for putting some money away every month in your wealth building account!

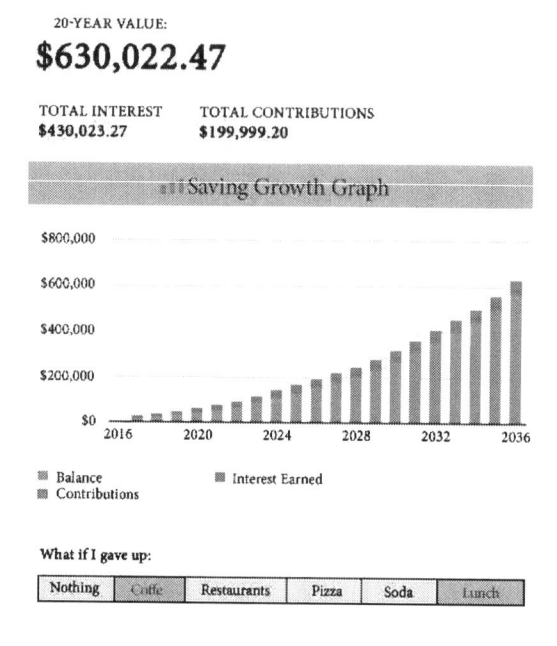

20-YEAR VALUE:
$630,022.47

TOTAL INTEREST: $430,023.27
TOTAL CONTRIBUTIONS: $199,999.20

Saving Growth Graph

■ Balance ■ Interest Earned
■ Contributions

What if I gave up: Nothing | Coffee | Restaurants | Pizza | Soda | Lunch

How would feel if you had a fresh well to drink from every day. Metaphorically speaking by sacrificing a little money now into a Roth Ira, mutual fund, or other investments you'll have your well when you need it most... In the later years of your life. I highly recommend you go make your own investing chart to see what your financial future could look like or speak with a qualified financial advisor. I like to follow Dave Ramsey, who has many resources on his website.

ACTION STEPS

▶ The next time you're at the bank set up your buckets, open different accounts.

▶ Always seek advice from a certified financial professional you trust and answers all your questions for starting a wealth building account.

▶ Schedule to get this done asap

Don't Be a Jerk to Your Older Self

Neurological studies have established that when most people envision their future self, they may as well be thinking of about an absolute stranger - someone they don't really care about. With these findings in mind, the scholars at The Journal of Marketing Research found a way to digitally age a person's image. Armed with these images they were able to ascertain that when people were able to accurately imagine their older selves, they began to care for themselves by setting aside significantly more money for retirement.

This was a study in "Temporal Discounting", whereby it has been found that people put a premium on immediate, short term gain rather than on future comfort and prosperity. Knowing this, be kind to your older self and:

> "Do not save what is left after spending, but spend what is left after saving."
> – Warren buffet

TOP TIP: If you're really serious about retiring wealthy, go to www.in20years.com where you can digitally age your face. Right after I saw what I looked 20 years from now I immediately called my financial advisor the next day and put a lump sum of money in my long term wealth building account. I recommend you print that photo out and hang it in your closet as motivation for saving for your future. Just looking at that photo of your older self will immediately change your perspective.

Giving Equals Abundance

From miraculous occurrences in nature we can learn lessons which, if acted upon, can change our lives and financial path. Think about how blessed we are to have air to breath, thanks to the process of photosynthesis. The air in some countries is so polluted that bottled air has become a valuable commodity.

Consider the miracle of trees. If you look closely at the pattern of the seasons you can observe trees growing abundantly, changing colors, then dropping their leaves. These leaves then decay near the base of the tree, nourishing the roots, the tree trunk, and in turn making the branches stronger. The fallen leaves are a gift to the tree. By giving back to itself, the tree grows more strong and taller the following year. You're probably thinking, "How does all of this relate to sacrifice?"

Maybe you already give a portion of your income or your time to the less fortunate. If you do, please know that this pureness of intention will help to catapult you in the direction of your best life ever. Giving without expecting anything in return is the highest form of excellence.

Action Steps

▶ Identify your marshmallow. What do you need to sacrifice to take your life to the next level?

▶ Get to work: Take massive action and work smart, equipped with a calendar and deadlines to help you achieve your goals.

▶ Form little habits which have the potential to help you become a better version of yourself?

▶ Set up an automatic saving plan so that you can start paying yourself first. This will ensure that you will retire in comfort.
☒ Give often, even if it's only a little:

> *"At the end of the day it's not about what you have or even what you've accomplished… It's about who you've lifted up, who you've made better. It's about what you've given back".*
> **– Denzel Washington**

By making small sacrifices in life you will empower yourself. Your ultimate purpose is become the best version of yourself. If you follow the simple tips in this chapter, you will be able to create the kind of life most only dream of.

Chapter 11

Making V.I.S.I.O.N.S Work For You

MAKING V.I.S.I.O.N.S WORK FOR YOU

PUTTING DAILY VISIONS™ TO WORK

So what's the next step? We went over the action steps on how you need to; create your wheel of life to know where you are today, write a list of your dreams, place your dreams on a vision board and then block out time to achieve all the areas you want to conquer in your life. The fuel that will spark massive results for your action steps are going to be; practicing your daily visualizations or meditations, specific intentions towards each goal, empowering your subconscious to stay inspired, and acting on opportunities that will come your way. You need to make your dreams and the actions that will get you to achieve them as non-negotiables for your life. There will be things that happen along the way that will try to distract you from your dreams, but you will be equipped to sacrifice a little pleasure now for a lot of results in the future.

Sequence of Action Steps:

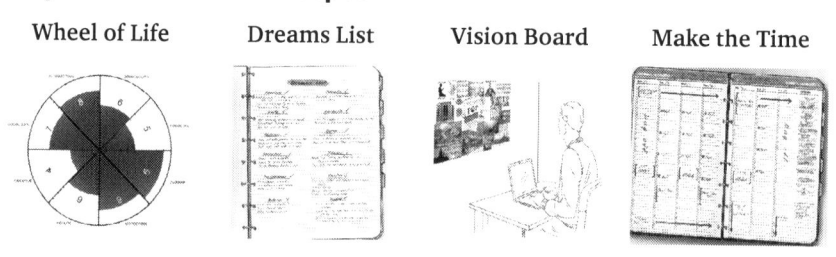

| Wheel of Life | Dreams List | Vision Board | Make the Time |

You've received the message of this book loud and clear, and are ready to conquer the world and take on your dream life. How do you tap into you're DAILY VISIONS™ in the most efficient way possible? Let's take a look back at what you've learned so you can put DAILY VISIONS™ to work immediately.

YOUR PERSONAL LIFE

Use DAILY VISIONS™ to give you laser-like focus in the most important areas of your life. Here are suggestions for where this focus should be directed:

• In your visualization, what images do you see at the moment of your success, what feelings do you feel, and what do you hear at this moment?

• What goal do you have your intention set to, to be drawn in through magnetic energy?

• What seeds is your subconscious currently growing? What abundance are you intentionally meditating towards?

• How much are you sacrificing each week from your paycheck to be able to live wealthy later?

YOUR FAMILY

Let the DAILY VISIONS™ acronym increase your overall happiness and ensure that you have great experiences with the ones you love. Here are few questions you can ask yourself to help get you started.

- What moments do you visualize for this month that will improve your relationships?
- How can you be more intentional with all your loved ones? How can inspiration play a role with your parents or children?
- What sacrifices do you need to make in your life in order to bring joy to those you love?
- The examples above may not represent what is most important to you. If you can benefit from them, great. Otherwise find ones which are more meaningful to you.

Remember to keep a calendar, or some other sort of organizer, to keep track of the most important task of the day which you want to knock off first. Place your biggest rocks in your bucket bright and early. Don't get caught up with busy work -

focus your efforts on productive tasks which bring you closer to your goals. For an added challenge, try timing yourself during each task.

Get to work using DAILY VISIONS™ in your personal and family life and begin to notice exciting changes emerge.

YOUR JOB

Put DAILY VISIONS™ to the test in your business life in order to achieve incredible results. There is magic in believing, so expect results. Get started by answering these questions:

- What opportunities can you take advantage of that are right in front of you but on which you've not yet pulled the trigger?
- Where can you put up a vision board to help tap into your inspiration?
- Which dreams will you attempt from your Non-Negotiable dreams list? • What would you wish to achieve in business if you knew you couldn't possibly fail? Use Visualization, the power of focused intention, and subconscious programing through meditation to ignite the fuse towards that dream, then take daily action.
- Who can you share DAILY VISIONS™ with that will appreciate it?

YOUR WORK TEAM

Introduce DAILY VISIONS™ the next time you're speaking with others at work. Whether it's an assistant, the manager, or the owner everybody can benefit from becoming a better version of themselves. Here are some situations to consider.

- While sitting with a team of sales people, give them a dreams list assignment to fill out and put in their calendar, so that they will have a clear vision of what they are working towards.

Sometimes sales people focus only on numbers, and burn out in the process. Their energy would be more sustainable if they had a greater understanding of their purpose.
- How can you encourage others to sacrifice a little income over the next 5 to 20 years in order to invest in a wealth building account?
- At any small gathering, seize the opportunity to ask, "What area in your life is giving you the most inspiration at the moment?"

There are any number of other strategies which you could come up with in order to show your team that you care about them. Seeing that these are not just words, but strategies you use in your own life will motivate people to move in the right direction.

Whether exposed to DAILY VISIONS™ in a casual discussion or an organized workshop, co-workers, sales people, and management will soon be coming up with creative ideas of their own. When people become aware of exactly what they want in life, passion will begin to flow through them, and business will thrive.

If applying DAILY VISIONS™ in different sectors of your business requires a number of participations, consider providing everyone with their own copy of the book. Sharing your "aha" moments together will be motivating for team members, and you may be pleasantly surprised at the results once they have read the book and understood it.

Understand that it will take more than a few fleeting conversations and meetings for some people to make DAILY VISIONS™ a new habit. There is some dispute over how long it takes to form a habit, but I gravitate towards the University College of London study from 2009 which found that it takes approximately 66 days. So approach your team with patience.

Chapter 12
Time to Thrive

Time To Thrive

It's Your Turn to Thrive!

By reading this book, you without a doubt want to start living aligned with your biggest dreams, and on your way to becoming your best self. If you walk the path exactly how I've laid out the bricks in this book, you will certainly achieve your goals faster than you ever believed possible. I guarantee it!

I wrote this book because I wanted to share the DAILY VISIONS™ technique so that people could begin getting precisely what they want out of life, and get in the "game", instead of continuing to coast along on the sidelines.

If you follow this blueprint you will experience what has helped so many others across the globe head straight for their dreams. The next steps are up to you. The key is for you to take action. Are you willing to make a positive commitment to yourself? The door is open; will you walk through?

If I can go from a poor background and almost losing my hand to becoming healthy, wealthy, and happy, so you can you.

If 23-year-old Jacob can go from making only $2k per month working 30 hours a week to making $15k per month working 24 hours a week, so can you.

If Teddy can go from broke to wealthy, with a penthouse and a Bentley, so can you.

If Trevor and Lisa can imagine their dream home and a month later be in it, so can you.

If Matt can intentionally set his life up to win a Rolex for being a top performer, so can you.

If a man can walk into a Starbucks with a mindset of abundance and walk out with a business deal, so can you.

You may have to miss some TV shows, movies and late nights hanging out with your friends, but the opportunities and new adventures that will show up in your life will far outweigh these.

I could have continued rolling on, enjoying my breezy life, smashing my competition with ease and keeping these secrets to myself, but I have a larger purpose.

I am sharing my DAILY VISIONS™ in this book to help people create a designer life, which will enable them to leave a legacy of wealth for generations to come.

You've hand selected this book for a reason. It ignited your interest because of your desire for a better life, or because you believe you have more to share and achieve. Whatever your driving force is, face life head on with intention and purpose in order to make a lasting impression on the world.

It's your turn to Thrive!

I look forward to hearing your stories of victory and success!

I hope that you will send me a letter, postcard, or note once you achieve some exciting moments from your dreams list. Let me know how your life has been more enriched as the result of using DAILY VISIONS™

You can reach me *Justin@VisionsToTheTop.com*

Here's to your designer life!

– **Justin Ledford**

Thank You for Reading My Book!

I sincerely appreciate all of your helpful feedback, and would love to hear what you say.

Your testimonials are what will help to make the next version even better.

Please leave me a supportive review by going to my Amazon book listing www.VisionsToTheTopBook.com and tell me what you think in a review

Always Grateful!!!
- **Justin Ledford**

About the Author

JUSTIN has achieved high levels of success in 4 different industries before the age of 30. He is a Hall of Fame salesperson with Millions of dollars in direct sales. He has simultaneously built a marketing organization of over 4,500 people, a construction company that produces over 1 Million in sales annually and is an active real estate investor. He speaks frequently at personal growth seminars sharing his mastery of how to achieve BIG goals while living a dream fulfilled life.

Justin and his team have the skills to help people from all walks of life overcome any challenge. Whether a person is looking to make more money, become more balanced, or take their life to next level, his passion is to help others thrive.

Alongside his business success, Justin and his wife/business partner, Sara, spend several months each year traveling. They are both advocates of sustainable living and holistic health.

Reach out to him at *www.JustinLedford.net*, or connect with him on:

Twitter: *https://twitter.com/JustLedford*
Facebook: *https://www.facebook.com/JustinOLedford*

Notes

Chapter 3

U.S. Census Bureau, Saperston Companies, Bankrate. January 3rd, 2016. Statistic Brain Research Institute. Web. 21 Feb 2016.

Chapter 4

Schmalbruch, Sarah. Here's The Trick Olympic Athletes Use To Achieve Their Goals. Business Insider. Jan 28, 2015 Business Insider Inc. 25 Jan 2016

Stone, Avery. Kerri Walsh Jennings says no pressure for Rio Olympics. February 23, 2015. USA TODAY. 25 Feb 2016.

Williams Anna. 8 Successful People Who Use The Power Of Visualization. MBG Editorial Team. July 8, 2015. Mind Body Green. 25 Feb 2016.

Pillay, Srinivasan MD. The Science of Visualization: Maximizing Your Brain's Potential During The Recession. Huffpost Healthy Living. November 17 2011. Huffington Post. 29 Jan 2016

Chapter 5

Emoto, Masuro MD. The True Power of Water and Love Thyself. Carlsbad. Hay House Inc. 2004

"Dasrath Manjhi" Wikipedia, The Free Encyclopedia. Wikimedia Foundation, Inc. 17 August 2007. Web. 10 Jan. 20016.

Carney, Dana, Cuddy, Amy, Yap, Andy. Power Posing: Brief Nonverbal Displays Affect Neuroendocrine Levels and Risk

Tolerance. Association for Psychological Science. Online First. 2010 Web. 25 Feb 2016.

Chapter 6

Abarracin, Dolores, Senay, Ibrahim, Noguchi, Kenji. Social Cognitive Influences on Specific Behavioral Patterns. Social Action Lab at the University of Illinois at Urbana-Champaign. 2001. Web. 28 Feb 2016.

Chapter 10

Casey, B. J., et al. (2011). Behavioral and neural correlates of delay of gratification 40 years later. Proceedings of the National Academy of Sciences.

Written by Justin Ledford
Copyright: 2016 Justin Ledford

Made in the USA
San Bernardino, CA
03 May 2017